Scotland's Landscapes
The National Collection of
Aerial Photography

James Crawford

Scotland's Landscapes

The National Collection of Aerial Photography

Royal Commission on the
Ancient and Historical
Monuments of Scotland

Published in 2012 by the
Royal Commission on the Ancient and
Historical Monuments of Scotland.

Royal Commission on the Ancient and
Historical Monuments of Scotland (RCAHMS)
John Sinclair House
16 Bernard Terrace
Edinburgh EH8 9NX

telephone +44 (0) 131 662 1456
info@rcahms.gov.uk
www.rcahms.gov.uk

Registered Charity SC026749

British Library Cataloguing-in-Publication Data.
A catalogue record for this book is available
from the British Library.

ISBN 9781902419824

Frontispiece: Amid a colourful landscape of
coastal grasses and peat on the Isle of Lewis,
lines of abandoned cultivation surround a
group of ruined stone huts. DP109580 2011

Series design by Dalrymple
Layout and typesetting by Tilley&Tilley
Typeset in Brunel, Frutiger and Minion
Printed in Poland by OZGraf

Royal
Commission on the
Ancient and
Historical
Monuments of
Scotland

Contents

Introduction

In the spring of 1788, the physician and naturalist Dr James Hutton set sail from the harbour of Dunglass in East Lothian, on a mission to examine at close range the curious rock formations on the south-east coast of Scotland. Hutton was accompanied on his short expedition by John Playfair, Professor of Mathematics at the University of Edinburgh, and Sir James Hall, President of the Royal Society of Edinburgh. All three were leading figures of the Scottish Enlightenment: gentlemen of science who applied logic and reason to the obscure mysteries of how the world worked. On a day of fine weather and calm seas they sailed south-eastwards along the Berwickshire coastline to the serrated cliffs of the promontory of Siccar Point.

As they approached the shore, and then landed below the cliffs, Hutton explained to his companions the intricacies of how these rocks had been formed – explaining, in essence, a new science called 'geology'. Rather than buried underneath ordered layers of sediment at the bottom of an ocean, this stretch of coast had, over a vast expanse of time, been bent, crushed and propelled upwards by immeasurable force. Here was proof, Hutton said, that the earth was not thousands of years old – as the Bible told them – but millions. Playfair later recalled that, 'The mind seemed to grow giddy by looking so far into the abyss of time; and while we listened with earnestness and admiration to the philosopher who was now unfolding these wonderful events, we became sensible how much farther reason may sometimes go than imagination can venture to follow.'

Scotland's earliest ancestors arrive into Hutton's story some 10,000 years ago. As a warming climate brought on the end of the last Ice Age, seas flooded the coastal gouges sculpted by innumerable glaciers, and huge quantities of melt water turned giant rocky troughs and the worn grooves of ancient fault lines into lochs. Gradually the land was swathed in forests of pine, oak, aspen, elm, birch, juniper and lime – a dense cloak alive with deer, elk, boar, fox, bear and wildcat. At first, it was hunter-gatherers that ventured into this wild, abundant territory. But over time, our ancestors decided to stay for good – to farm and to build.

In the low light just after dawn, beyond the still waters of Loch Quoich, the jagged mountains of the Knoydart peninsula catch the sun. In the distance, the islands of Eigg and Rum are still shadows on the horizon. Here is a landscape seemingly without human intervention – one that captures a sense of what Scotland may have looked like some 10,000 years ago, as the melting glaciers and rising sea levels inundated the western seaboard. The reality, however, is rather different. In 1955, the North of Scotland Hydro Electric Board dammed the eastern end of Loch Quoich, raising its water level by over 100ft and increasing its surface area from 3 to 7 square miles. In the process, the extensive remains of eighteenth century farming settlements and Victorian shooting lodges were drowned beneath a man-made 'flood'.

DP110076 2011

From the very beginning, people were making Scotland's landscapes. And they have continued to do so ever since. Hutton revealed a history of the world that stretched back millions of years. But landscapes are a product of human invention and intervention. The word 'landscape' itself has two origins – first as a medieval phrase for enclosed, man-made spaces, and then, from the Dutch in the sixteenth century, as a painter's term referring to a pleasing view. And so landscapes mean different things to different people, and are as much a product of our minds and our experiences as they are expanses of stone, earth and water. The hunters who arrived as the glaciers melted saw a landscape of opportunity. The first farmers, who began to clear the 'wild woods', saw a landscape of rich, fertile soil. The societies who created some of our earliest architecture – massive stone tombs and circles built in alignment with the sun, moon and stars – saw the landscape as a bridge to an afterlife. Millennia later, the philosophers of the Enlightenment judged the landscape as a resource to be changed and 'improved' for the sake of progress and productivity. The artists, poets and writers of the late eighteenth century pictured the landscape as the setting for poignant history and sublime romance. And the engineers of the Victorian era took the landscape on as a challenge – terrain to be bridged, tunnelled and crossed, as a symbol of man's all-conquering ingenuity.

Through the National Collection of Aerial Photography, we can journey above Scotland – looking down on islands and mountains, sweeping over undulating lowlands, and tracing the intricate outlines of an unmistakable coast. These are modern landscapes – snapshots of the here and now. But if we look closely enough we can read the long and complex histories of how they came to be. Time and man have left indelible marks, but there is one constant in the life of a landscape – change. The landscapes of today will never be the landscapes of the future. With every passing day, month, decade and century, layers continue to be added and erased from the landscape story of Scotland. It remains a remarkable, dramatic and fascinating story, a story that Hutton himself concluded had 'no vestige of a beginning – no prospect of an end.'

A thin trail of mist hangs above the 'King's Pass' in the valley of the River Tay. This pastoral landscape is almost entirely the creation of man. As the A9 curves through a patchwork of 'improved' farmland, the surrounding hills are covered by the trees of Craigvinean Forest, one of the oldest managed forests in Scotland. Craigvinean was grown originally from larch seed brought from the Alps by the Second Duke of Atholl, and was part of the great expansion of forestry in the eighteenth and early nineteenth centuries in Perthshire. Between 1738 and 1830, the 'Planting' Dukes grew some 27 million conifers – 'for beauty and profit' – around Dunkeld, reputedly even using cannons to help scatter the seed.
DP056565 2008

Islands

In August 2001, a team of archaeologists working among the coastal dunes of the Taobh Tuath peninsula on the Isle of Harris made a remarkable discovery. Drilling boreholes down several metres into the machair – the wind-blown, sand and peat grasslands that dominate the Atlantic fringes of the Outer Hebrides – they recovered the unmistakable traces of man: flint and quartz, charred grain, hazelnut shells and substantial amounts of animal bone. It was a prehistoric rubbish dump, a pile of detritus left behind long ago and submerged for many centuries deep within the soil. There was nothing immediately unique or unusual about this find. But with carbon dating, its true significance emerged. This jumble of discarded fragments was over 9,000 years old – the first proof that people had reached as far as the Western Isles this early in the human story of Scotland. Sometime around 7000 BC, hunter-gatherers had moved northwards through a warming landscape freed from the grip of the last Ice Age, and made landfall on Harris.

It is often in the nature of archaeology that the thread of history is followed best through what has been thrown away. Abandoned hunting implements and millennia-old camp sites – just like the one on Harris – can help plot the advance of ancient nomadic communities along the length of the western seaboard. We now know that, with the glaciers finally melted away, hunter-gatherers spread throughout the islands of Scotland, from Islay, Jura and Colonsay in the south, to Rum, Skye and Harris in the north. At first, these were family-sized groups who migrated with the seasons, leaving only fleeting evidence of their passing as they navigated the distinctive spine of coastlines, mountains and sea lochs. Over time, however, the nomadic lifestyle was replaced by permanent settlement and the development of farming. And from that moment on, people began to write their story firmly into the fabric of the island landscapes.

In the modern imagination, Scotland's islands are often thought of as wild and lonely places. In fact, the landscapes that we see today are the product of 10,000 years of near continuous human activity. And for the vast majority of this time-span, the defining characteristics of island life have not been solitude and isolation, but connections and community. Imagining the Scottish island seaways of 3000 BC, Vere Gordon Childe, the renowned Chair of Prehistoric Archaeology at the University of Edinburgh from 1927 to 1946, described a kind of northern European Polynesia, with 'grey waters as bright with Neolithic argonauts as the western Pacific is today.'

That is not to say, however, that island landscapes are the same as those on the mainland. In fact, the specific physical nature of islands – a 'knowable' body of land surrounded by water – may have inspired some of our most unique and advanced prehistoric communities. Around 5,000 years ago, a number of Scottish islands were central hubs with trading links across the sea to Ireland, England, Scandinavia and even further afield. And the vibrant cultures that thrived in these places produced some of our first true architectural masterworks. The Neolithic Orcadians in particular transformed the spaces around their homes and farms into a vast landscape of ritual and ceremony. Giant stone circles and tombs were built to be visible for miles around, part of a society that appears to have been preoccupied intensely with death and religion. Indeed, the sheer volume of monuments constructed on Orkney during the third millennium BC – many of which remain standing to this day – have made it one of the most remarkable and enigmatic sites of the entire ancient world.

Yet almost every period of Scotland's history has left its imprint on the island landscapes. Some traces are buried in the dunes, or overlie each other in complex patterns; others have erased completely what has gone before. By discovering and studying what has been left behind, we continue to learn more about our islands. From the stone remains of Iron Age 'brochs', to Viking boat timbers and abandoned concrete machine-gun emplacements, there is a millennia-long story of defence, conquest and conflict. The spread of Christianity from the islands to the rest of Scotland can be followed from sixth century monasteries and isolated chapels to medieval parish kirks which have witnessed generations of worship and burial. And patchwork crofting townships, stone 'enclosure' dykes, and roofless, ruined farmhouses, demonstrate the human impact on the landscape of the eighteenth and nineteenth century 'improvement' lairds, who looked to turn their island holdings into profit.

These scattered remains are the vocabulary of island history. Put together they form a shifting narrative of adventure, culture, innovation, faith, war, loss and redemption. We have made and unmade our islands many times, and will continue to do so in the future, as modern communities explore new ways of managing the landscape. But there is something heartening in knowing that our islands retain the memory of our earliest presence, however faint. That if we look hard enough, we can travel all the way back to Scotland's human beginning, to our earliest ancestors first landing on a deserted beach, making camp, and striking out into the unknown to hunt and explore.

PREVIOUS PAGES
This colourful crofting patchwork at the Taobh Tuath peninsula on the Isle of Harris overlies the machair landscape where the buried debris of a near 9,000-year-old hunter-gatherer camp was discovered. In the nineteenth century, farmers working this fertile shoreline were evicted and forced to eke out an existence on the rocky and inhospitable east coast of the island – where the soil was reputedly so thin that crops could not be sown and it was impossible even to bury the dead. It was only after the First World War, when the government bought much of the machairs of the west coast, that the community returned to live and work on the land.
DP110522 2011

RIGHT
Thin trails of early-morning mist hang above the waters of Loch Grimshader on the east coast of the Isle of Lewis. On the shorelines modern communities occupy a landscape littered with the remains of earlier buildings, field boundaries and cultivation.
DP111269 2011

TOP LEFT

On the half land, half water landscape of the eastern seaboard of Lewis, 'lochan' pools of peaty water fill the glacial troughs scoured out between knolls of Lewisian gneiss. Formed around 3,000 million years ago, these rocks are among the oldest to be found anywhere in the world – and there is certainly nothing beyond their age in the geological record of Scotland. Stretching out from Loch Buaile Bhig, this broken plateau of rock and peat has provided the islanders with an abundant source of fuel for millennia.

DP111264 2011

BOTTOM LEFT

In June 1980, archaeologists found two Bronze Age burial chambers – one containing the bones of an adult and the other an adolescent or young adult – partly exposed above the dunes of this rocky bay at Traigh Bhan on Islay. The first body was buried over 3,500 years ago, and the second another 200 years later. Islay is a rich source of evidence for early human activity in Scotland, and just a few kilometres from Traigh Bhan, near the Bowmore whisky distillery, an 11,000-year-old flint arrowhead was discovered – a clear sign that people had been exploring and hunting in the landscapes of Scotland immediately after the last Ice Age.

DP046388 2008

RIGHT

For millennia a settlement has lain buried beneath the extensive dunes at the Links of Noltland on the Orkney island of Westray. This 5,000-year-old site was rediscovered in the 1980s, after storms, gales and erosion had scoured the coastal landscape to reveal the faint traces of buildings. Yet perhaps the most remarkable find on the site came in 2009, when excavators unearthed a small, sandstone figurine, complete with markings intended to represent a face and clothing. Dubbed the 'Orkney Venus', or the 'Westray Wife', this 3.5cm by 3cm carving is the earliest known representation of a human form ever found in Scotland.

DP068313 2009

Looking out to the vast expanse of the
Atlantic Ocean, the rocky, wave-lashed
sand bay at Magnersta on the west coast
of Lewis is a picture of remoteness.
Here, in low winter sunlight, the distinctive,
sinuous ridges of former cultivation emerge
alongside the fragmentary outlines of ruined
buildings and stone dykes – the remnants
of an early nineteenth century township.
Yet this is no abandoned landscape – the
village of Mangersta and its 9,000 acres
of common grazings remain in use to
this day by the residents of a modern
crofting community.

DP110807 2011

Around the small settlement of Cromer on
the east coast of Lewis, roads and houses
crest the rocky uprisings between watery
pools and inlets in a chaotic landscape.
Beyond, Loch Eireasort plunges into the
heart of the island. This deep valley was
scoured out of the rock of Lewis by the
glaciers of the last Ice Age, before being
inundated many thousands of years ago
by rising sea levels.

DP109546 2000

LEFT

At the south-west corner of South Uist, in a part-submerged landscape below the bare mound of Beinn Ruigh Choinnich, is the ferry port of Lochboisdale – which succeeded Loch Skipport as the island's principal harbour in 1900. Just emerging from the haze on the horizon is the serrated outline of the Cuillin mountain range on the Isle of Skye. D110538 2011

ABOVE

With its name taken from the Gaelic *Lios Mòr*, meaning 'great garden', the fertile limestone island of Lismore points south-west out of Loch Linnhe, past Mull, to the open sea. Settled from prehistoric times, it would become a centre of Celtic Christianity after the missionary monk St Moluag founded a monastery on the island around AD 562.

In the mid nineteenth century, in common with so many other areas of Scotland, a new landowner seeking better financial return from his holdings evicted the crofters and cottars from the southern half of Lismore. In their place, he created a depopulated landscape of criss-crossing enclosure walls dedicated to sheep farming. DP017747 2006

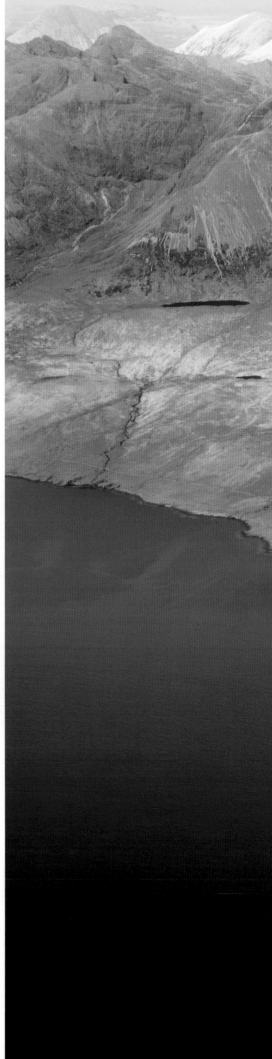

Reached today by a lonely track from the road junction at Glen Brittle, the Rubh' an Dunain peninsula on the Isle of Skye has been a place of human activity for millennia – from our earliest hunter-gatherer ancestors to settlements occupied as recently as the 1860s. Perhaps most interesting of all is Loch na h-Airde at the promontory's tip, a lochan once connected to the sea by a man-made cutting known as the 'Viking canal'.

Timbers of a 900-year-old Norse boat were discovered here, along with a stone quay and a control-system to keep the water level constant. Archaeologists believe this may have been the site of a medieval shipyard and naval base, where boats were built and secured during the harsh winter months: an ingenious use of a natural feature.

ABOVE **DP098280** 2010

RIGHT **DP109392** 2010

Covering the very last square metres of land at Berneray's southernmost tip are two buildings separated by over 2,000 years: a massive drystone wall, probably dating to the Iron Age, and the nineteenth century Barra Head lighthouse, designed by the famous Stevenson dynasty of engineers. This island, which has been occupied from prehistoric times right up until the lighthouse keepers finally left in 1980, is the last, rocky footprint of the Hebridean archipelago. With no shallow waters to the west, it is also the first breaking point for Atlantic storms, and fish have reputedly been thrown the full 190m height of its cliffs to land within the walled enclosure of the keepers' cottages and graveyard.

DP110565 2011

ABOVE

Taken from the old Norse meaning 'flat island', Fladda and its lighthouse sit at the heart of the 'slate islands' of Seil, Easdale, Luing, Lunga, Shuna, Torsa and Belnahua in the Firth of Lorne. This tiny archipelago was quarried heavily for roofing materials during the nineteenth and early twentieth centuries.

DP017987 2000

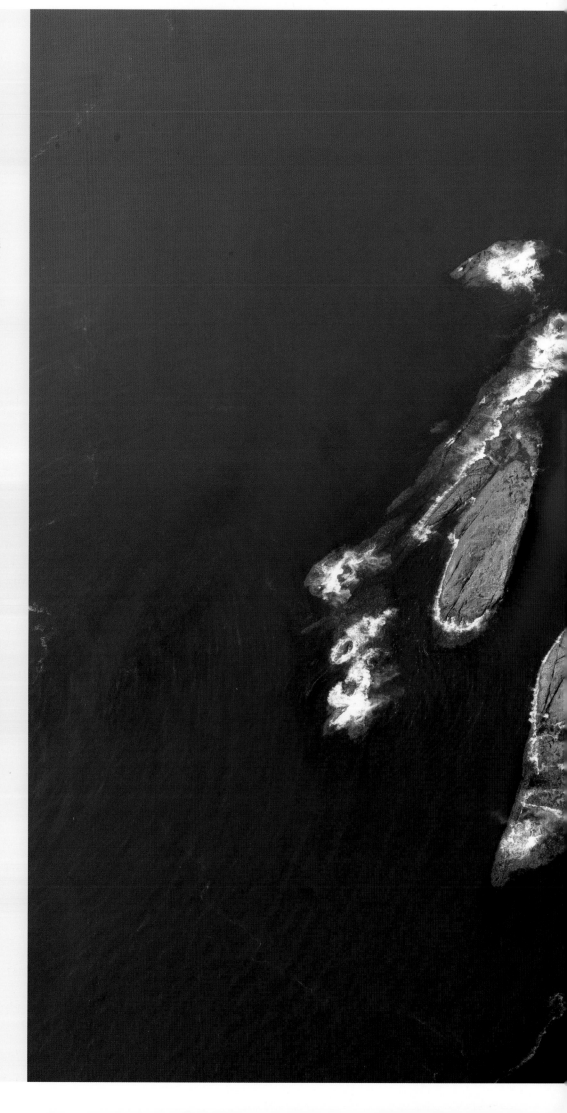

Built in 1904 to a design by Charles and
David Stevenson, the 39m-high Hyskeir
lighthouse lies in the southern entrance
to the Minch to the west of Rum, and warns
approaching ships of the Mills Rocks and
the Isle of Canna. One of the last lighthouses
in Scotland to remain manned – it was only
automated in 1997 – it was once famous
for a one hole golf course created by its
keepers. The construction of lighthouses
across the islands and coastlines of
Scotland required mastery of landscapes
and engineering – involving erecting, on
barren Atlantic rocks, structures capable
of enduring the relentless onslaught of
wind, wave, tide and weather. Between 1790
and 1940, eight members of one family –
the Stevensons – planned, designed and
constructed 97 towers to punctuate the
Scottish seaboard. As the famous writer
and family-member Robert Louis
Stevenson remarked, 'when the lights
come out at sundown along the shores of
Scotland, I am proud to think they burn
more brightly for the genius of my father.'
Once these beacons were in place, they
created a new landscape – a network of
navigation points that aided safe passage at
all times and in all weathers. As technology
has moved on, however, the question arises
as to whether or not the time of these
structures has passed. As the biographer,
of the Stevenson family, Bella Bathurst
writes, 'Somewhere out there, past the
back of beyond will be a neat white wall,
a few wind-scoured cottages and a tower …
If you remember that these light squares
are now abandoned, perhaps they seem
more like graveyards. All that stone and
history and effort, you think, just for
a lightbulb.'

DP109425 2011

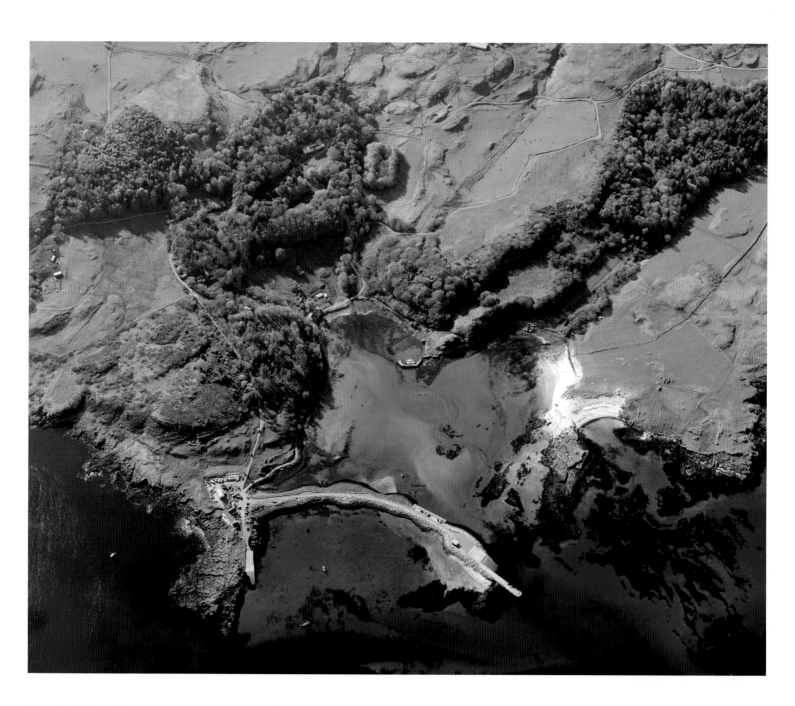

The island of Eigg's main harbour at the head of Galmisdale Bay bears the name of its owners from the late medieval period to the early nineteenth century – Clanranald. The clan chiefs were forced to sell the island in 1828, and from then on, Eigg passed from one wealthy absentee landowner to another – including a Scottish military doctor, a Danish ship-magnate and an enigmatic German artist and property speculator. Finally, in 1997, the island was bought by its own community in the form of the Isle of Eigg Heritage Trust. This approach is beginning to transform how landscapes are managed across Scotland. In 2004, as one of the measures taken by the Trust to improve access to Eigg, the harbour, whose first pier was built in 1790, had its jetty extended to allow for the docking of large ferries.

DP109446 2011

Following the gentle crescent of the village of Kerrycroy on the east coast of the Isle of Bute, a small, red-rubble sandstone quay arcs out into the bay. This harbour is one of many small anchorages on the shores of the island, along with those at Straad, Kilchattan, Port Bannatyne and Kilmichael.

First built at the beginning of the nineteenth century, Kerrycroy was – until the construction of the Rothesay pier – the site of the ferry connection to Largs, and the most significant link between Bute and the mainland.

DP066005 2009

Looking out towards the Sound of Harris from the island's fjorded southern coastline, the harbour of Leverburgh was established by Lord Leverhume in the early twentieth century as a large-scale fishing station. Leverhume's intention was to bring industrialisation to the Harris economy but, despite investing £1.4 million of his own fortune in the island, little remains of his attempt to re-engineer the landscape. After his death in 1925, the Leverburgh project was abandoned and all that is left among today's modern village is a water tower and reservoir, the foundations of a powerhouse, coopering sheds and fisher girls' quarters.

DP110639 2011

First built in 1800, and reconstructed in 1885, the Port of Ness harbour was described in 1852 by the Ordnance Survey as 'one of the principal fishing stations in the island of Lewis', with the main types of catch listed as ling, cod, haddock and herring.

DP111216 2011

With a white spume of water at its stern, a ferry begins to move away from Port Aiskaig on IsIay to navigate the narrow channel alongside the Isle of Jura. Between 2006 and 2009, the nineteenth century harbour was redeveloped at a cost of nearly £14 million, demonstrating the economic importance of a modern transport infrastructure to connect local communities and help tourists reach the island landscapes.

DP112327 2011

Connected to the mainland in 1995 by
a concrete road bridge curving over the
waters of Kyle Akin, the question has
been asked – does Skye remain a true island
after such major human intervention?
Some suggest that the notion of 'boundary'
is key to an island's existence and identity,
and that physical bridges challenge
islanders' sense of themselves, their past,
and their future. Island landscapes are
defined by the idea of segmentation, yet
also, at the same time, by connections –
by their essential links to the outside world.
Perhaps a bridge may threaten an island's
existence, or perhaps it may save it.
Interestingly, studies have shown that the
population of Skye has grown since the
construction of its bridge. Of course, few
islands have as strong a 'brand' as Skye,
from its historical links to Prince Charlie
and the Rebellion, to its iconic geology –
seen here in the dramatic peaks of the
Cuillins on the horizon.

DP109900 2011

At the head of Loch Cheann Chuisil on
the west coast of Lewis, a track winds
away from the remains of an abandoned
township through the red-hued rocks of
Gleann Tamnasbhal. Largely the preserve
of hill walkers today, this route once
connected the inhabitants of Cheann
Chuisil to the coastal plain and the
townships to the north.

DP110791 2011

The houses and crofting strips of the
townships of Cros and Ness cluster
alongside the main road to the Port
of Ness and the Butt of Lewis – the
most north-easterly point of the island.
Many buildings here overlie the remains
of previous communities. The 1852
Ordnance Survey Object Name Book
records it as 'A large village of huts
through which passes the road leading
from Stornoway to Ness. They are built of
stone and earth and thatched with straw …
There is a large tract of good arable land
and some indifferent moorland. Attached
to it is a tract of the best land in Lewis.'

DP111187 2011

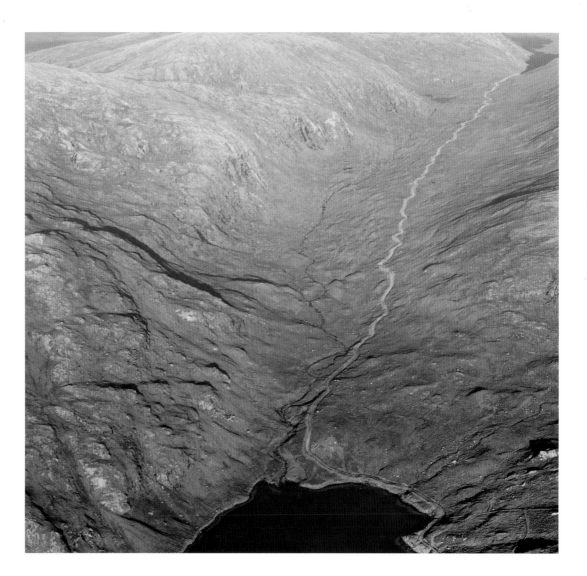

Overlooking Loch Roag to the west of
Lewis, the standing stones of Callanish
are part of a ritual landscape dating back
5,000 years. Believed in the seventeenth
century to be 'false men' turned to stone
by an enchanter, the uprights of this
enigmatic monument today rise above
modern housing and the hard line of
an enclosure wall. DP110872 2011

ABOVE

Above sheer cliffs on the Orkney island
of South Ronaldsay, a path leads to a
dark hole in a hillock of wildgrass.
Just broad enough to fit a man lying flat,
this narrow, stone-built passageway –
navigable by stretching out on a wheeled
trolley and pulling along a rope – opens out
to an enlarged chamber. It is a journey of
just four metres, but also of 5,000 years:

a portal between the present day and
Scotland's ancient past. A burial site
for the bones of 340 people, this was
also a ceremonial space, filled with
tools, pottery, jewellery and the remains
of the totemic, white-tailed birds that
colonised these Orkney cliffs and give
this place its name – the Tomb of
the Eagles. DP068044 2009

LEFT

On the Atlantic coastline of Lewis, the crumbling remains of the medieval chapel of Teampull Eion and its enclosed cemetery stand out a lush, striking green against the surrounding landscape. First built in the fifteenth century, the abandoned churchyard contains over 2,000 unmarked gravestones.

DP109574 2011

ABOVE

On the north-east coast of Orkney Mainland, the tight square of another graveyard – and site of the now ruined St Nicholas' Chapel – sits angled against the ordered geometry of a modern field pattern.

DP068255 2009

ABOVE

The remains of Dun Mor Vaul broch on Tiree appear as two near-perfect concentric stone rings. When first built about 2,000 years ago, this stronghold on the island's Atlantic coast reached many metres skywards. Excavations at the site have revealed remarkable artefacts, including Roman glass bowls and dice fashioned out of solid bone. DP094609 2010

RIGHT

Kisimul Castle on Barra was first built in the fifteenth century to demonstrate ownership of its surroundings – both the land and the seaways. A home for the clan chief of the MacNeils of Barra, it continued to guard the entry to Castlebay until it was gutted by fire in 1795.

Soon after, the island's thriving herring fishing fleet began taking the castle's stones to use as ballast for their boats. Kisimul was rebuilt in the twentieth century, and in the year 2000 the current clan chief Ian MacNeil granted the castle to Historic Scotland on a 1,000 year lease – with an annual rent of £1 and a bottle of whisky.

DP110590 2011

During the Second World War, the entire Orkney archipelago was transformed into an impassable barricade, as four causeways cut off seaborne approaches to the major Royal Naval base at Scapa Flow. Between 1940 and 1942, nearly 2,000 men – half of whom were Italian prisoners-of-war – created the defences by setting huge concrete blocks on top of rubble foundations laid across the sea bed.

Once complete, the 'Churchill Barriers' created artificial links between Orkney Mainland and the islands of Lamb Holm, Glimps Holm, Burray and South Ronaldsy. After the war a road surface was laid across the causeways, establishing a permanent transport connection to the south-eastern corner of the Orkneys.

ABOVE DP067970 2009
RIGHT DP067974 2009

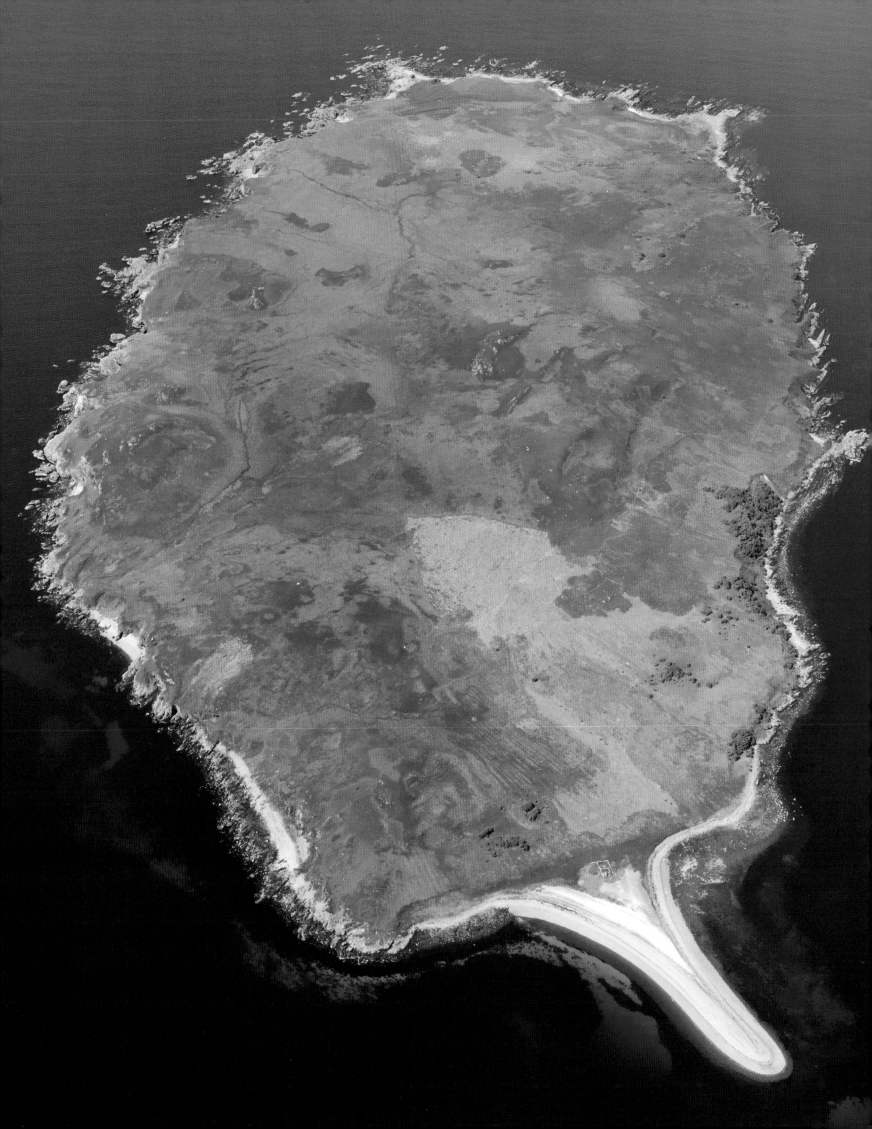

In 1942, military scientists arrived on Gruinard Island in the Highlands to conduct a 'top secret' experiment. Sixty sheep were transported to the island and exposed to the contents of a series of gas canisters. This was the test site for a potentially lethal biological weapon – anthrax. The whole flock was wiped out in days, and Gruinard was deemed a 'no-go' area for over 50 years. In 1990, after being soaked in formaldehyde and seawater, it was declared free from contamination – but it remains a forbidding place. Perhaps most chilling was the conclusion reached by the Second World War report: anthrax could be used to render cities uninhabitable 'for generations'. DP093124 2010

Inchmickery in the Firth of Forth is a relic of both conflict and peace. Used as a gun battery during the First and Second World Wars, it is today a protected breeding ground for rare Roseate terns.
ABOVE RIGHT DP049268 2008
BELOW RIGHT DP076442 2010

A storm beach separates a lochan from the sea here at Sandig on the east coast of Lewis, an active process set alongside the slow decay of buildings and fields abandoned more than 150 years ago. The first edition of the Ordnance Survey 6-inch map of Lewis, published in 1854, recorded two roofed buildings, and one unroofed structure on the site – evidence perhaps of a settlement already deserted or in decline. Sir James Matheson, owner of Lewis for much of the nineteenth century, had persuaded the Ordnance Survey that areas of Scotland in need of agricultural improvement should be made a priority for mapping. He paid the extra expenses required to ensure that his island landscape was surveyed ahead of schedule and out of sequence – the intention had been for the Ordnance Survey to move northwards systematically from the lowlands – agreeing at the same time to purchase 100 copies of the maps once they were complete.

DP109567 2011

A flight over the Outer Hebrides reveals a landscape that has undergone quite incredible change since the end of the last Ice Age. Over millennia, the sea has consumed the 'long island' – the collective name for the rocky, fish-like backbone stretching from Lewis in the north, through Harris and the Uists, and ending at the flicked tail of Barra, Mingulay and Berneray. Around 11,500 years ago, the sea was over 50m below its present level, and the land stretched west into the Atlantic. Local folklore even holds that the seabed between Lewis and St Kilda was once the hunting forest of a Hebridean princess. Today, the Atlantic rushes through the channels of the 'long island's' spine to the Minch, and the erosion and submersion of the landscape continues. Hand in hand are the processes of human movement and abandonment, which leave behind their own vivid patterns. Here at Uamh'a Ghobha on the north-east coast of Lewis, three roofless nineteenth century houses cling to the cliffs, with one standing beside the remains of the ancient promontory fort of Dun Bhilascleiter.

DP111238 2000

Cut off from the main body of Harris, Scarp is a mountain islet formed by Beinn fo Thuath rising steeply out of the sea. This flat ledge of cultivable land on its eastern fringe was the site of a crofting township, whose population reached a peak of 213 people in 1861. Less than a hundred years later, however, this had fallen to 74, and in 1971 the last family left the island and its scattered spread of buildings – including a chapel, schoolhouse and mission house. Scarp is perhaps most famous to the wider world as the site in 1934 of a German sceintist's ill-fated attempt to pioneer the world's first 'rocket-mail' postal service.

DP110773 2011

Above the ivory sands of the beach of Traigh Mhor on the east coast of Lewis, the sunlight picks out the patterns of 'lazy-bed' cultivation ridges and long-disused enclosures.

DP111251 2011

Lit a vibrant orange-green by a low winter-sun, the tightly bunched humps and shadows of abandoned 'lazy-bed' cultivation ridges are divided by a turf dyke – a boundary between two adjacent farming townships which leads down to the sands of Port Sto at the Butt of Lewis. The First Edition of the Ordnance Survey 6-inch map of the island recorded a building annotated as a 'Fish House' positioned just above the shoreline of the Port, but no obvious remains are visible today.

DP109585 2011

This collection of roofless ruins clustered at the knuckle joint of a sheer cliff peninsula on the Shetland island of South Havra, forms the remains of a small fishing community. In 1923 the island, whose low hill-peak was once topped by Shetland's only windmill, was abandoned by its last eight families.

Life was reputedly so hazardous here that both children and animals had to be tethered to prevent them falling over the cliffs. DP081268 2010

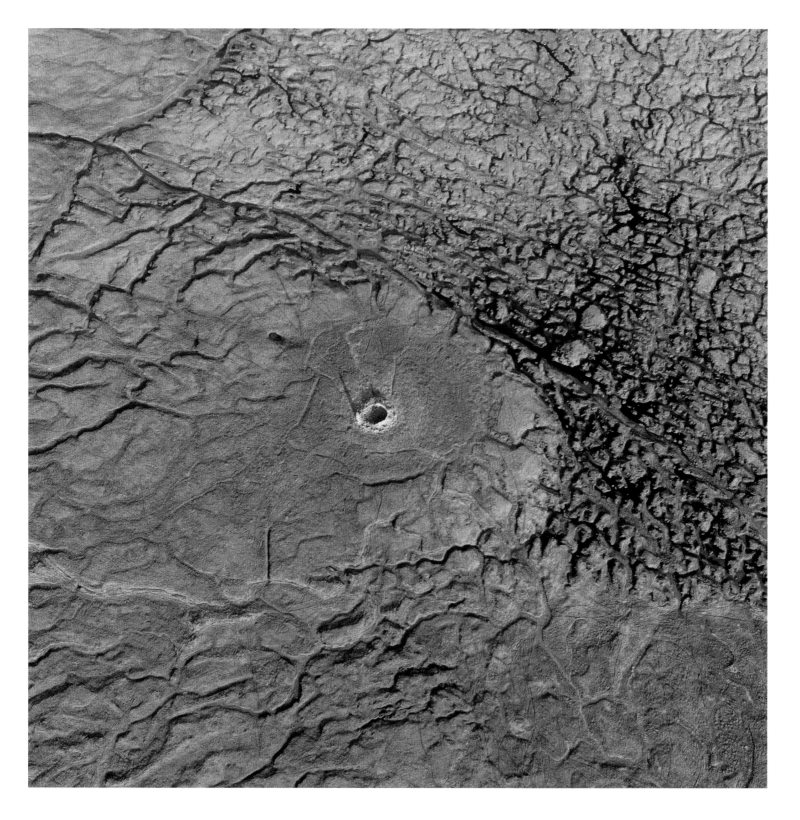

Looking as much like the surface of
Mars as the coastal peat-flats of Lewis,
a wrinkled red landscape converges around
the disintegrated stub of Dun Borve broch.
Much of the original structure, built many
centuries ago, now lies buried beneath
the rising peat, and in more recent times
there is evidence that it was reused as
an animal pen. DP109581 2011

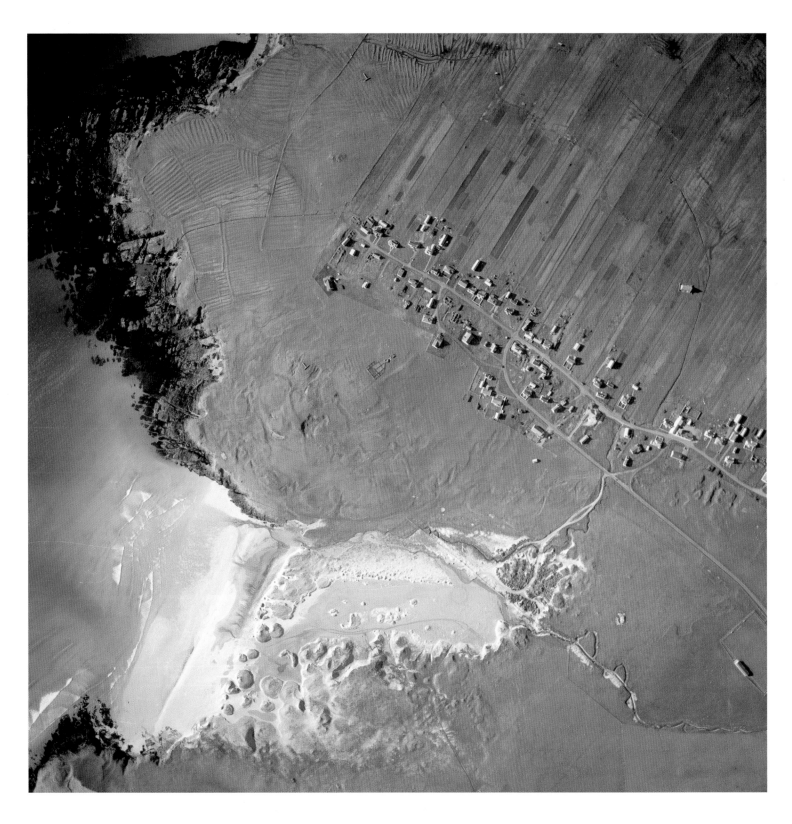

At the southern tip of the Outer Hebrides, Vatersay has been a home to people for thousands of years, with ancient remains ranging from an Iron Age fort to a 5,000-year-old chambered burial cairn. Life continues to thrive on the island today, helped by the opening in 1991 of a road-surfaced causeway linking Vatersay to Barra. DP110585 2011

The 1852 Ordnance Survey Object Name Book described the township of Eoropie as, 'A village of huts built of stone and clay, and thatched with straw. It is the most northerly village in Lewis, situated on a patch of good arable land, which is very much impoverished by the sand being blown over it from the shore in stormy weather.'

While traces of earlier farming remain visible above the rocky coast, stretching inland are strips of crofts still worked today by this modern, 'improved' township. SC748822 1994

Surrounded by bone-white sands and a
cobalt sea is the small crofting community
of Luskentyre on the south-west coast
of Harris. As with other tenants of the
machair lands, the crofters who lived here
in the mid nineteenth century were evicted
by the then owner of the island and
replaced by sheep farms. Despite their
removal from the land, the community
continued to bury their dead in the
graveyard at Luskentyre, crossing
from their new holdings on the rocky,
inhospitable east coast, and creating tracks
across the mountains that became known
as 'coffin roads'. After the First World War,
the land was bought by the government,
and the crofts and farms were reinstated.
In January 2010, Luskentyre – along with
the estates of Borve and Scaristavore –
was purchased by the community, through
the West Harris Trust.

DP110664 2011

Beyond the waters of the Kilbrannan Sound, the snow-capped mountains of Arran surge up above the coastline. Often referred to as 'Scotland in miniature', Arran is split in two by the ancient Highland Boundary Fault. The southern half of the island is the population centre, a rolling landscape of villages and farmlands. The north, on the other hand, is a collosal mass of volcanic granite, carved by the glaciers into the rugged 'Highlands' we see today. In the late eighteenth century, Arran's unique landscape played a key role in the development of James Hutton's fledgling science of geology. In 1787, Hutton visited the island as part of the research for his groundbreaking work *Theory of the Earth*. Describing the expedition, his friend and biographer John Playfair remarked that Arran is, 'one of those spots in which nature has collected, within a very small compass, all the phenomena most interesting to a geologist.' Hutton, he wrote, 'returned from his tour highly gratified, and used often to say that he had nowhere found his expectations so much exceeded, as in the grand and instructive apearances with which nature has adorned this little island.'

DP056758 2008

Descending from a corrie on the west side of Beinn Bharrain, Allt Gobhlatch has cut deep into the rock of the mountainside. A village was established here in the eighteenth century by the cotton traders J & P Clarks of Paisely, with the fast flowing waters of the gorge used to power a pirn mill – a mill which harvested the woodlands to make bobbins.

In 1840, with the supply of trees from the surrounding landscape exhuasted, the mill was closed. Yet the village – still known as Pirnmill – has remained as a patchwork of farms and houses stretching along Arran's secluded north-west coastline.

DP056902 2008

Below the three rounded peaks of Beinn an Oir, Beinn a' Chaolais and Beinn Shiantaidh – the famous 'Paps of Jura' – the Glenbatrick River runs down to Loch Tarbert, passing on its way a solitary building. Facing out across the sands of an otherwise empty bay, this house was constructed in the nineteenth century as a hunting lodge. Jura – the name thought to come from the Old Norse, meaning 'deer island' – has long been a hunting ground, and prehistoric arrowheads and cooking-pits have been discovered at this same site. Today the whale-shaped, heather-clad expanse of Jura is home to around 5,000 deer, and every year between August and October hunters take to the hills for the stalking season.

ABOVE DP095594 2010

RIGHT DP031609 2010

Kinloch, at the head of Loch Scresort, is the only sheltered landing on Rum's 28-mile coast. In the 1980s, a stone arrowhead was discovered here along with the remains of ancient fires and hearthstones – revealing this bay as a 9,000-year-old hunter-gatherer camp and one of the earliest known 'settlements' in Scotland. Hunting has defined the history of Rum's dark, mountainous landscape. In 1888, it was purchased for use as a sporting estate, and became known as the 'Forbidden Isle', an exclusive play-park of the rich, with hillsides alive with herds of red deer. The castle of Kinloch, built in 1900, was described by Sir John Betjeman as a 'living memorial to the stalking, the fishing and the sailing, the tenantry and plenty of the days before 1914 and the collapse of the world'.

LEFT DP094939 2010
ABOVE DP094952 2010

ABOVE

On the southern tip of the Orkney Island of
Sanday, alongside the ferry terminal to Eday,
Stronsay and Kirkwall, a three-turbine
windfarm spreads out across the headland
of Spurness. With the wind a near constant
presence on Orkney, it is an appropriate place
to test the potential of renewable energy to
help create eco-friendly island landscapes.
DP055791 2009

RIGHT

There is no exact age for the sea stack
known as the Old Man of Hoy, although it
is speculated that it is less than 400 years
old. It does not feature in the first Atlas
of Scotland drawn by Timothy Pont in
the sixteenth century, but a sketch by the
landscape painter William Daniell in
1819 shows a two-legged stone upright
close to the form we now recognise.

Today, the stack has been transformed into a
challenge to the adventurous and the intrepid.
It was first climbed in 1966, and an RAF
logbook buried in a cairn on the summit
records the names of those who have
made the ascent since. With the continual
processes of erosion, what is certain is that,
one day, Hoy's iconic Old Man will collapse
into the sea. DP083412 2009

1
Taobh Tuath
peninsula,
Isle of Harris

2
Loch Grimshader,
Isle of Lewis

3
Loch Buaile Bhig,
Isle of Lewis

4
Traigh Bhan,
Islay

5
The Links of
Noltland, Westray,
Orkney Islands

6
Mangersta,
Isle of Lewis

7
Cromer,
Isle of Lewis

8
Lochboisdale,
South Uist

9
Lismore,
Loch Linnhe

10
Loch na h-Airde,
Isle of Skye

10
Rubh' an Dunain,
Isle of Skye

11
Barra Head
Lighthouse,
Berneray

12
Fladda Lighthouse,
Firth of Lorne

13
Hyskeir
Lighthouse,
The Minch

14
Clanranald
Harbour,
Isle of Eigg

15
Kerrycroy,
Isle of Bute

16
Leverburgh,
Isle of Harris

17
Port of Ness,
Isle of Lewis

18
Port Aiskaig,
Islay

19
Kyle Akin and
the Skye Bridge,
Isle of Skye

20
Loch Cheann
Chuisil,
Isle of Lewis

21
Cros and Ness,
Isle of Lewis

22
Callanish,
Isle of Lewis

23
The Tomb of
the Eagles,
South Ronaldsay,
Orkney Islands

24
Teampull Eion,
Isle of Lewis

25
St Nicholas'
Chapel,
Orkney Mainland

26
Dun Mor
Vaul Broch,
Tiree

27
Kisimul Castle,
Isle of Barra

28
The Churchill
Barriers,
Scapa Flow,
Orkney Islands

28
The Churchill
Barriers,
Scapa Flow,
Orkney Islands

29
Gruinard Island,
Wester Ross

30
Inchmickery,
Firth of Forth

30
Inchmickery,
Firth of Forth

31
Sandig,
Isle of Lewis

32
Uamh'a Ghobha,
Isle of Lewis

33
Scarp,
Isle of Harris

34
Traigh Mhor,
Isle of Lewis

35
Port Sto,
Isle of Lewis

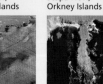

36
South Havra,
Shetland Isles

37
Dun Borve Broch,
Isle of Lewis

38
Isle of Vatersay

39
Eoropie,
Isle of Lewis

40
Luskentyre,
Isle of Harris

41
Isle of Arran

41
Pirnmill, Isle of
Arran

42
Glenbatrick,
Loch Tarbert,
Isle of Jura

42
Glenbatrick Lodge,
Loch Tarbert,
Isle of Jura

43
Kinloch,
Loch Scresort,
Isle of Rum

43
Kinloch,
Loch Scresort,
Isle of Rum

44
Spurness,
Sanday,
Orkney Islands

45
The Old Man
of Hoy,
Orkney Islands

Islands Locations

An endless interplay of form and pattern – seas breaking on deserted bays, dark mountain ridges caught in silhouette by the evening sun, glinting strands between land and water – Scotland's islands provide a remarkable palette for the aerial photographer. Aerial survey is about searching for clues from the past in shapes and shadows on the ground, as well as recording contemporary landscapes.

The unique quality of Scotland's light, changing at will with the weather and the seasons, can throw the familiar and the mundane into a rich tapestry of textures. In a split second, the aerial image can capture everything from the activity of an individual person in the here and now, to evidence of lives lived many thousands of years ago.

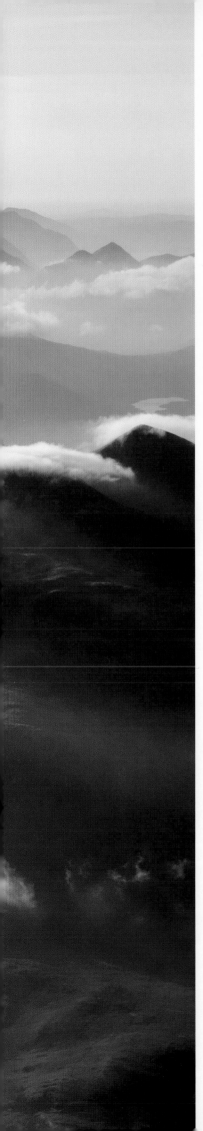

Highlands

In the summer of 1747, William Roy, the 21-year-old son of a Lanarkshire estate factor, stepped through the gates of Fort Augustus and looked out across the waters of Loch Ness. Roy was standing at the centre of the long geological funnel of mountains and lochs known as the Great Glen, and his destination was Inverness, some 38 miles to the north-east. As he set off, he placed a staff in the ground, walked ahead to the first bend in the road, and positioned another. Aided by a compass-like device known as a 'circumferentor' and pushing a surveyor's wheel, he measured the angle and distance between the two points, wrote the details in his notebook, and then repeated the process with the next bend. At the same time, he recorded the landscape features around him – rivers, paths, farmhouses, walls and fields – estimating their range from where he stood, and adding them to a sketch drawing of the route. He would continue this painstaking process all the way to Inverness. Single-handedly, Roy completed the opening leg of an almost unimaginably daunting task – producing the first ever ground-measured map of the Highlands of Scotland.

For the next year, he continued this process on his own, edging with meticulous care through harsh weather and unforgiving terrain. In 1748, his endeavours were supplemented by extra manpower, and soon six survey parties of six men each were taking their measurements across the Highland landscape. After another four years of assiduous application and remarkable endurance, the task was complete. 15,000 square miles of the Scottish Highlands had been mapped. When Roy and his men returned to Edinburgh in 1752, every recorded road, village, croft, mountain, glen, loch, beach and river was translated into a spectacular patchwork of northern Scotland – a series of ink and watercolour-wash maps produced to a scale of one inch to every 1,000 yards.

What had prompted such an arduous and complex undertaking? The answer to this question – at least initially – is unequivocal: civil war. During the Jacobite Rebellion of 1745 and 1746, the Hanoverian commanders in Scotland had found themselves 'greatly embarrassed for want of a proper Survey of the Country'. The Highlands were an unreadable *terra incognita* to the armies of George II, and both the conflict and the subsequent pursuit of the rebels were hampered by basic deficiencies in knowledge and understanding of the terrain. In effect, the landscape was an enemy. The geological border with the Lowlands was also seen as a political border – lochs and mountains were natural barriers and defences, and secluded glens were the cradle for fiercely independent clan communities. Some even concluded, rather feverishly, that it was the Highlands themselves, as much as the people that lived there, that were responsible for the Rebellion.

Not uncommonly in the history of cartography, this map-making was about a display of power, ownership, authority and control. Roy's 'Military Survey', as it was known, was intended to subdue an entire landscape by recording its every detail.

Yet there was more going on here than the martial pacification of northern Scotland. Roy was a man of science, not war. He pursued his task with the attention to detail and dedication to empirical truth that were the hallmarks of the Enlightenment. He proved that thought, reason and innovation could conquer a landscape – and rather than a political act, the goal was the pursuit of knowledge. While Roy made maps to better understand the patterns of the earth, he was not immune to another new way of seeing the landscape. Despite the extremes of toil and drudgery involved in his survey, he could still recall standing on the remote Coigach peninsula in Wester Ross and being confronted by 'a scene the most wild and romantic that can be imagined.' For those moments, the man of reason saw the world not as a series of measurements, but as a thing of joy and wonder.

Roy's work – which led on to the establishment of the Ordnance Survey – has played a key role in changing how we look at the Highlands today. The process of mapping the landscape was about control, even as it moved from military tool to Enlightenment benchmark. Yet once the task was completed, there was no legislating for how people would respond to the results. At the start of the nineteenth century, as the Romantic Movement swept through Europe, maps became a canvas for the imagination, and symbols of the freedom of the individual. In Scotland they opened up a perceived wilderness and provided direct routes back to nature. Rather than removing the mystique of the Highlands, maps have helped to accentuate it. The extreme geology and the poignant history of the region have combined to create a tourist magnet, a place to roam free in contemplation of the picturesque.

It is difficult to overstate just how much the perception of this landscape has changed over the last two hundred and fifty years. The supposedly barren, unknowable, dissident hotbed of the mid eighteenth century has been broken down into its component parts and reassembled as a patchwork of heights, distances, and tight, swirling contour lines. And in our modern world these intricate details and measurements, first put down in a military notebook by Roy, are transformed into a universally acknowledged vision of landscape beauty.

PREVIOUS PAGES
As early as the mid nineteenth century, pioneering photographers began taking their equipment into the sky in hot air balloons. For the first time, they were able to capture the physical reality of the top-down view that had been employed for hundreds of years by cartographers like William Roy. Just as maps are open to interpretation – Roy's military maps became an important first step in the origin story of the Ordnance Survey – equally there is no accounting for how people today will respond to an aerial photograph. In this image, taken early on a winter's morning, the sun cuts through the mists above Loch Treig, and in the distance the mountains around Mamore Forest and Rannoch Moor emerge as ghostly silhouettes. To the modern viewer, this photograph could capture the sublime romance of a 'wild' and 'lonely' landscape, or perhaps even evoke the atmosphere of a prehistoric dawn. During Roy's time and the Rebellion, however, the Hanoverians saw in the Highlands only 'rugged, rocky mountains, having a multiplicity of cavities … most adapted to concealment of all kinds'. As one newspaper wrote of the landscape, 'there are hiding places enough'.
DP110074 2011

RIGHT
A mixture of sunlit gold and heavy shadow, the angular peaks of the mountains around Glenshiel and Kinlochhourn corrugate towards the western-Highland coastline where Loch Hourn meets the Sound of Sleat. Just visible on the horizon are the dark shapes of the islands of Canna and Rum.
DP110077 2011

Beyond the rounded summit of Cnoc
Coinnich, with the peaks of The Cobbler
and Beinn Ime in the distance, the
increasingly imposing mountains of
the 'Arrochar Alps' mark the rise of the
Highlands above the western Lowlands.
A landscape carved by the glaciers of the
last Ice Age, this triangle of rock and forest
between Loch Goil and Loch Long makes
up the publicly owned Ardgoil Estate.
In 1905, the Liberal Member of Parliament
for Glasgow Tradeston bought the land and
gifted it to the City of Glasgow, writing to
the Lord Provost that his fellow citizens,
'should have a mountain territory which
will be their own for all time … My general
object is to preserve a grand and rugged
region for the best use of those who love
the freedom of the mountains and wild
natural beauty'.

DP057344 2000

At the head of Loch Torridon, in a landscape of jagged sandstone and quartzite, the slopes of Liathach are consumed by wildfire. The mountainside is pictured here in May 2011, when dry, warm conditions and strong winds saw blazes race through the gorse and heather of large tracts of the north-west Highlands.

Helicopters were employed to mount rescue operations, and to drop water bombs in an attempt to tackle the spread of the fires.

ABOVE DP109968 2011
RIGHT DP109959 2011

Between the sandstone pinnacle of Slioch and the waters of Loch Maree is the lush township of Letterewe. Transformed in the nineteenth century into an agricultural settlement, this was once the site of one of Scotland's first ever 'industrial' ironworks – with a charcoal-fired blast furnace depicted in 1610 on John Speed's *'Map of the Kingdome of Scotland'*. Today, the remains of this early industrial centre lie scattered alongside the 'Furnace Burn', seen here running from Loch Garbhaig in the middle-distance down to Loch Maree.

DP074687 2009

The village of Ballachulish imposes an ordered grid of roads, fields and housing over the fjord landscape beyond the mouth of Glencoe. As early as 1693, slate quarrying began here, and by the twentieth century, Ballachulish was producing over 26 million slates every year. In 1818 Thomas Larkin described in his *Sketch of a tour in the Highlands of Scotland* how 'the quarry is most conveniently situated for sea carriage, the waters of Loch Leven washing the side of the mountain from which a pier stretches into the lake. To the end of this pier may be lashed vessels of considerable burden, into which the slates are thrown from hand-barrows rolled from the quarry; so that on the same spot the article is raised from the ground, manufactured, and shipped for any quarter of the world.' Larkin was impressed by the oppositions in this landscape, noting how 'the crowd, the activity, noise, and bustling industry of this place, contrast agreeably with the stillness, solitude and silence of the scene behind'.

DP026762 2007

Surrounded by high mountains in the remote reaches of Wester Ross, this private hunting lodge sits on the northern bank of Loch Fannich, a tiny, manicured oasis at the centre of an otherwise uninhabited valley.

DP074554 2009

At the entrance to Glenshiel, the Cluanie Inn has acted as a rest stop for travellers since it was first built in 1787. Between 1725 and 1740 – as a response to Jacobite uprisings – the military officer George Wade embarked on a major engineering project to 'open up' the landscape of the Highlands to government troops. The construction of 250 miles of 'military roads' linked the army bases of Fort Augustus, Fort William, Bernera and Ruthven. Built on a foundation of boulders and then covered by stones and gravel, the roads tackled the landscape head on, ascending vertiginous slopes, winding through high passes, and diving down mountainsides. As Samuel Johnson wrote of a journey on the roads, 'to make this way … might have broken the perseverance of a Roman legion'. Wade's successor William Caulfield extended the network, and by 1767 over 1,000 miles crossed the Highlands. Here, the remains of the road from Fort Augustus to Bernera, built by Caulfield in 1755, are just visible beyond the Inn and the modern A87. DP111915 2011

A solitary track curves towards Cluanie Lodge on the banks of Loch Cluanie. In 1957 the construction of a dam and hydro-electric scheme here created an entirely new landscape, raising the waters of the loch by 29m. DP111913 2011

Dark cloudbanks loom over the head of Loch Fyne and the small village of Cairndow. In 1803, the poet Dorothy Wordsworth journeyed from Cairndow's stagecoach inn around the banks of the loch, recalling that, 'Our road never carried us far from the lake, and with the beating of the waves, the sparkling sunshiny water, boats, the opposite hills, and, on the side on which we travelled, the chance cottages, the coppice woods, and common business of the fields, the ride could not but be amusing.' Wordsworth's book of her travels, *Recollections of a Tour Made in Scotland*, became a classic of nineteenth century travel literature, and had a major influence on the popular transformation of the Highlands into a 'romantic' and 'picturesque' landscape.

DP057340 2008

In this winter view of Glen Lochay, the snowline ends just as the surrounding funnel of mountains meets the pasturelands in the river valley. The first edition of the Ordnance Survey 6-inch map for Perthshire, published in 1867, recorded a substantial farming township near the head of the glen. Today, the most prominent remnant of this settlement is Moirlanich longhouse, a wonderfully preserved farm cottage and byre built in the mid nineteenth century. Just below the longhouse is the large, bulky cube of an electricity substation, connected to Lochay Power Station further up the valley – once the control centre for the entire Breadalbane Hydro-Electric Scheme.

DP086753 2010

The first novel Queen Victoria ever read was Walter Scott's *The Bride of Lammermoor*. Charmed by the romantic storylines, she was even heard to describe herself as a 'Jacobite at heart'. It was the Highland landscape in particular that captured her imagination, and in 1848 she purchased Balmoral on Deeside. Over the coming years Victoria and her husband Prince Albert transformed Balmoral into their principal residence in Scotland. This royal Highland estate popularised a romantic version of Scottishness, and led to a new architectural style called the Scots Baronial. Mock-medieval turrets, battlements and towers appeared on buildings from country houses to town halls and hospitals. But beyond the architecture, this nostalgia industry also had a profound effect on the landscape. Scott's poem *The Lady of the Lake*, a favourite of Prince Albert's, reintroduced the heroic image of the hunting monarch. Throughout the later nineteenth century, the traditional Highland landscape was cleared not for sheep farming, but to create vast tracts of 'wild' land managed for deer, grouse, trout and salmon – Highland 'theme parks' for the aristocratic and the rich.

LEFT DP020832 2004
ABOVE DP020828 2004

Built in the thirteenth century by the Comyns of Badenoch – a powerful Scottish dynasty whose lands stretched from Argyll in the west to Buchan in the east – Lochindorb Castle's strategic importance is not immediately obvious. Today, it feels particularly remote: a tiny island in a loch surrounded by bare moorland. Yet 900 years ago, the castle was at the centre of a forest, and archaeologists now suspect that Lochindorb was a hunting lodge for the Comyn family and their noble guests. In 1302, as Edward I looked to secure the support of the local aristocracy for war in Scotland, he was hosted at the castle – evidence perhaps that, more than just a defensive stronghold, here was a structure and a landscape designed for hospitality and entertaining.

LEFT DP098372 2011
ABOVE DP098380 2011

Opposite the village of St Fillans at the east end of Loch Earn, Neish Island is probably a man-made feature of the landscape – although the exact date of its construction is unknown. The island was both a residence and bolthole for the Clan Neish from the mid thirteenth century until its inhabitants reputedly met a gruesome end at the hands of their local rivals. Published between 1882 and 1885, the *Ordnance Gazetteer of Scotland* records that, 'In the early part of the seventeenth century the small remnant of the clan Neish … subsisted on this isle by plundering, till, one winter night, they were surprised and slain – all save one man and a boy – by their ancient foes, the Macnabs.' Local legend holds that, in retaliation for robbing a party of the Clan Macnab on the outskirts of Crieff, the Chief of the Macnabs and his twelve sons carried their own boat on their shoulders from Loch Tay, over the mountains around Glen Breich and through Glen Tarken, to the shores of Loch Earn. The Neishes were massacred in the ensuing raid, with only the two who stayed hidden surviving to tell the tale and carry on the family name.

LEFT DP051104 2008

ABOVE DP051105 2008

On an outwash fan created where the
waters of Allt Coire Mhicrail meet Loch
Hourn, the buildings of the substantial
eighteenth century crofting community
of Skiary are disintegrating slowly into
the landscape. Although the last family
left the township in 1950, the site has
still not been abandoned completely.
Amid the crumbling remains, one building
has been restored and is now run as a
guest house – accessible by taking the
22-mile-long single-track road from
Invergarry to Kinloch Hourn, and then
travelling by boat through Loch Beag
to the township shore.

DP111874 2011

In Strathfleet to the north of the Dornoch Firth in the northern Highlands, the earthwork remains of Little Rogart reveal a long history of farming going back many hundreds of years. When viewed from above in low, raking light, this long grassy ridge becomes an intricate pattern of abandoned cultivation rigs and the remains of farm-buildings, corn-drying kilns, and walled enclosures. Traces of stone-walled round houses show that the land was settled in prehistoric times – though the first written record of the site is a 'Hearth Tax' return dating to 1691, which records three tenants. By 1815 this had increased to fourteen, but soon after the inhabitants must have been cleared, as the township does not appear on an 1833 map of Sutherland. Instead, in its place, are two buildings enclosed by a stone dyke – seen here in the top right of the photograph. These are likely to be the house of a shepherd brought in to manage the surrounding landscape as an extensive sheep farm. DP080250 2009

TOP LEFT

Emerging from dense heather, this oval
of stones on the summit of Craig Obney
to the east of Glen Shee is all that remains
of a hillfort. Set in a commanding position
with views northwards to Strathbraan and
eastwards to the River Tay, this may have
been a seat of local power, built to display
authority over the surrounding landscape.

DP056564 2008

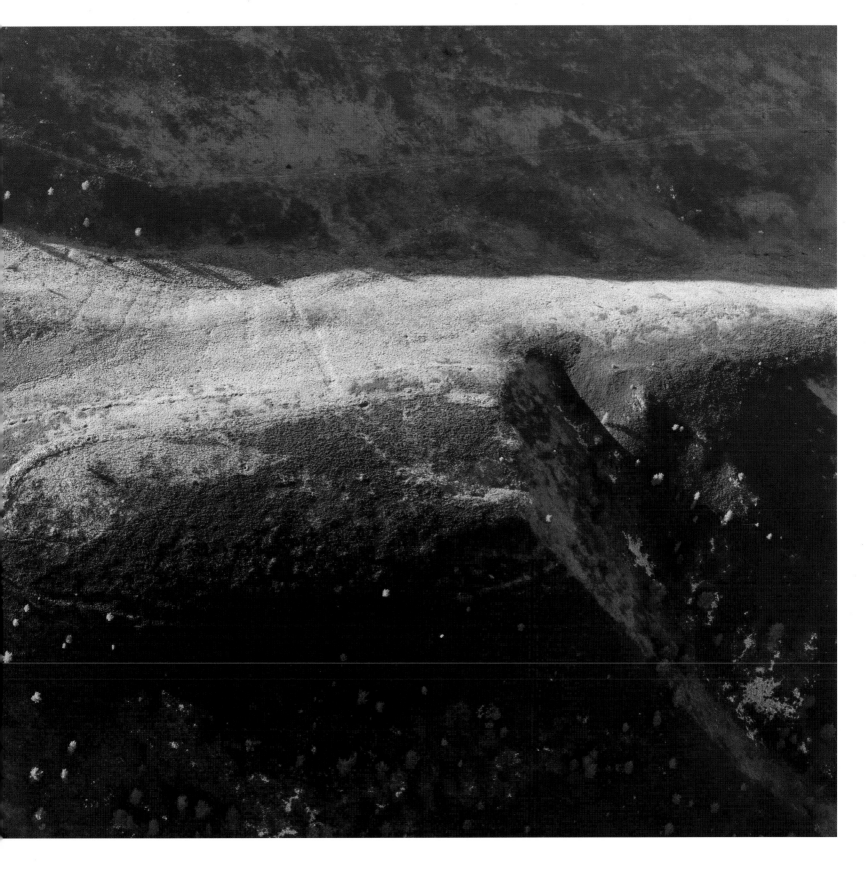

BOTTOM LEFT

Found at the heart of a now lonely moor in the Caithness flow country – the largest expanse of peatland bog in Europe – are two of the oldest stone structures still standing in Scotland. Over 5,000 years ago, the massive 'Grey Cairns' of Camster were built at the heart of this once fertile land, and held the remains of the Neolithic farmers who worked here –

before the advance of the deep blanket of peat. Pictured here is the 'long cairn', a 60m-long and 20m-wide stone tomb – its scale giving an insight into the extraordinary efforts made by our prehistoric ancestors to create sites for burial and ritual.

DP092204 2010

ABOVE

In the low light of a spring evening, the curves of two rocky walls form the faint thumbprint of Cnoc an Duin hillfort in Ross and Cromarty. Overlooking the west bank of the Strathrory river, Cnoc an Duin was built around 2,500 years ago – although archaeologists believe that, for some reason, the construction was never finished.

DP080274 2009

In 1904, construction began on the Blackwater Dam, a colossal concrete wall designed to turn an entire glen into an artificial loch. One of the first major hydro-electric projects undertaken in Scotland, this was a pioneering attempt by the British Aluminium Company to harness the innate power of the landscape in the service of heavy industry – in this case a large-scale aluminium smelting plant at Kinlochleven. It required landscape re-engineering on an epic scale. A workforce of 3,000 men took up residence in a temporary village on the desolate mountainscape above Rannoch Moor, their task to turn three small lochs and their tributary rivers into one massive body of water. The numbers involved were astounding. The dam was over half a mile long, 86 feet high and 62 feet thick at its base. On completion it was the longest dam in the world, and it transformed the valley into Blackwater Reservoir – 9 miles long, 75 feet deep, and eventually holding 24,000 million gallons of water.

The construction was a treacherous undertaking and accidents were common: many workers died from falling into excavation holes, or during dynamiting of the rock. Today, beyond the dam's battered downstream wall, you can still see the small, fenced plot of a navvies' graveyard, with headstones carved out of concrete construction blocks. The British Aluminium Company proved, without a doubt, that the lochs and rivers of the Highlands were an abundant source of power – the incredible scale of hydro-electric aluminium production in Scotland was sated only by the demands of the Great War. Yet it would be after the Second World War – when the Hydro Schemes returned on an even bigger and more ambitious scale than before – that the transformation of the Highlands into an 'energy' landscape truly began.

DP026733 2007

In 1812, on the orders of the Commission for Highland Roads and Bridges, the engineering pioneer Thomas Telford completed the construction of a road linking Fort William to Arisaig – now the modern A830. Less than a hundred years after Telford's achievement, a second route was built through the western Highlands to the coast, and this time it was made of iron.

The Fort William to Mallaig extension of the West Highland Railway brought steam trains through the remote landscapes of Scotland. It was here in 1901, at the head of Loch Shiel, that Robert McAlpine created one of the most iconic railway engineering structures found anywhere in the world – the great concrete curve of the 380m-long, 21-arch Glenfinnan Viaduct.

ABOVE **DP111847** 2011

Near Tomatin in the valley of Strathdearn, it was the railway that came first and the road that followed. In 1897 the Highland Railway Company laid a 400m-long steel girder viaduct over the River Findhorn on nine slender stone piers. It would be another 80 years before the present road bridge was built to carry the A9 over the same stretch of valley

RIGHT **DP074312** 2009

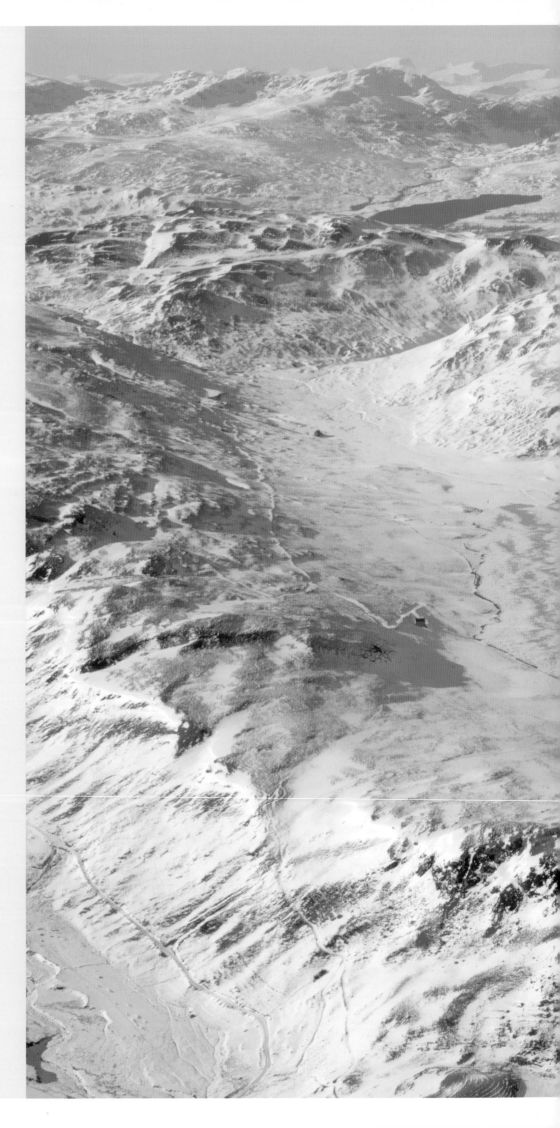

In the mountains above the Perthshire village of Comrie, the frozen Lednock Loch takes on the appearance of an Alpine glacier. The dam here was built in 1957, and is one of only two diamond-headed buttress dams in Scotland – its structure designed to resist the occasional earthquakes triggered by the nearby Highland Boundary Fault. In this second wave of Hydro Schemes, the goal was not just the generation of electricity, but also the economic and social regeneration of the Highlands. In 1941 Winston Churchill appointed Thomas Johnstone, a Labour Party veteran and committed socialist, as Secretary of State for Scotland. Johnstone took control of Scotland's vast water system, and saw in hydro-electric power the opportunity to transform the welfare of an entire region and its inhabitants – not for profit, but in the name of social equality. At that time, less than 1 per cent of people living outside the main settlements in the Highlands had electricity. Johnstone established the North of Scotland Hydro-Electricity Board in 1943, its coat of arms bearing the motto in Gaelic, 'Heart nan Gleann' – 'Power from the Glens'. Over the next three decades a series of monumental engineering projects turned this motto into a reality. Using the unique geology and climate of the landscape, the Hydro Board created one giant, interconnected power grid, bringing electricity to almost every croft, farmstead and household north of the Highland line.

DP086721 2010

On the very fringes of the north-east Highlands, a forestry plantation swathes the slopes of Bennachie. In 1503, the Scottish Parliament announced that the forests of Scotland were 'utterlie destroyit'. The history of trees in Scotland had up to that point been one of almost relentless decline.

The great Caledonian Forest emerged some 11,000 years ago, after the end of the last Ice Age, and had stretched across almost the entire landscape, as far even as Shetland and the Western Isles. But over millennia the dense carpet of birch, hazel, pine and oak was removed through human intervention and climate change.

By the time of the Roman invasion of Scotland in the first century AD, at least half of the natural woodland had disappeared, much of it replaced by moors of peat and bog. The pace of deforestation did not relent, and, despite the Parliament's recognition of the problem at the start of the sixteenth century, by 1900 forests covered less than 4 per cent of Scotland's total land area. DP011678 2005

Above Loch Lochy, the forest of South Laggan unfurls along the slopes of the Great Glen. Here, between the trees and the shoreline, the remains of General Wade's 1727 Fort William to Fort Augustus military road are clearly visible. It was along this road that William Roy walked alone in 1747 as he began his enormous task of surveying the Highlands. And it is thanks to Roy's maps, which also recorded the locations of forests, that we have arrived today at the definition of 'ancient woodland' as 'land that is currently wooded and has been continually wooded since at least 1750'. Scotland's forests reached their lowest ebb at the beginning of the twentieth century and, perhaps ironically, it was war that would spark the regeneration. In 1919, Lloyd George declared that Britain 'had more nearly lost the war for want of timber than of anything else'. As a result, the Forestry Commission was founded in the same year, with the explicit remit of arresting the decline. The result has been a major transformation of the modern landscape. Whereas at the start of the twentieth century, only 4 per cent of Scotland's total land area was woodland, today this figure has increased to just under 18 per cent. DP111929 2011

Here in the valley of Glen Croe, the steep, rocky slopes of Beinn Luibhean descend through the parallel routeways of the A83 and William Caulfield's Dumbarton to Inverary military road. This stretch of road, which rises to a pass 860ft above sea level, was first completed in 1748. To commemorate the arduous engineering works, a stone seat was erected on the summit bidding travellers to 'rest and be thankful'. Roads may have conquered the glen, but, for the Scottish judge Lord Cockburn writing in 1838, the landscape remained unbowed by the incursion of man: 'As I stood at the height of the road and gazed down on its strange course both ways, I could not help rejoicing that there was at least one place where railway and canals, and steamers, and all these devices for sinking hills and raising valleys, and introducing man and levels, and destroying solitude and nature, would for ever be set at defiance'.

DP099591 2011

Zig-zagging its way up a slope of grey scree is the 'pony track' built in 1883 to service the weather observatory on the summit of Ben Nevis. While the observatory – visible in ruins here by the cliff edge – was abandoned in 1904, the track remains the most popular route to the top of the mountain. In many ways, this image is symbolic of the popular transformation of the Highlands.

In 1891, Sir Hugh Munro of Lindertis published a table of all the peaks in Scotland above 3,000 ft. This list stretched to 248 – with Ben Nevis the highest – and ever since, outdoor enthusiasts have been rushing north of the Highland Boundary Fault to climb them. This pursuit of 'Munro-bagging' recasts ancient geology as one vast leisure park. The Scottish ecologist Fraser Darling called the

Highlands a 'wet desert' made barren by human intervention – but that is not what the majority see. As the French philosopher Roland Barthes put it, 'myths turn history into nature'. Today, inspired by the poignancy of the Highland story, the landscape is embraced as a perfect, picturesque wilderness – a place to walk, climb, explore and enjoy.

ABOVE DP094877 2010

RIGHT DP094871 2010

1
Loch Treig,
Lochaber

2
Kinlochhourn,
Sound of Sleat

3
Cnoc Coinnich,
Arrochar

4
Liathach,
Loch Torridon

4
Liathach,
Loch Torridon

5
Letterewe,
Loch Maree

6
Ballachulish,
Loch Leven

7
Fannich Lodge,
Loch Fannich,
Wester Ross

8
Cluanie Inn,
Glenshiel

9
Cluanie Lodge,
Loch Cluanie

10
Cairndow,
Loch Fyne

11
Glen Lochay,
Breadalbane

12
Balmoral Castle,
Royal Deeside

12
Balmoral Castle,
Royal Deeside

13
Lochindorb Castle,
Badenoch

13
Lochindorb Castle,
Badenoch

14
Neish Island,
Loch Earn

14
Neish Island,
Loch Earn

15
Skiary,
Loch Hourn

16
Little Rogart,
Strathfleet

17
Craig Obney,
Glen Shee

18
The 'Grey Cairns'
of Camster,
Caithness

19
Cnoc an Duin
hillfort, Ross
and Cromarty

20
Blackwater Dam,
Rannoch Moor

21
Glenfinnan
Viaduct

22
Tomatin Village,
Strathdearn

23
Lednock Dam,
Perthshire

24
Bennachie,
Aberdeenshire

25
South Laggan,
Loch Lochy

26
The 'Rest and
Be Thankful',
Glen Croe

27
Ben Nevis,
Lochaber

27
Ben Nevis,
Lochaber

Highlands Locations

Aerial survey and photography can often be a severe test of endurance – turbulence, cold air and a 100mph wind whipping through the cockpit can take their toll on even the most seasoned aviator. Communicating through their head-sets, the pilot and aerial photographer use concise commands to direct the Cessna 172 survey aircraft above the landscape.

Once they are close to a target, the plane banks tightly to the left – one wing pointing straight down towards a landscape some 2,000 feet below – and the passenger window is thrown open. In that moment, the cramped cockpit fills with wind and noise, and every 500th of a second, with a whirring click, high-resolution, digital images are written to a memory card.

Lowlands

In 1792, a 21-year-old Edinburgh lawyer, left with a permanent limp after a bout of polio as an infant, embarked on a walking tour of the Scottish Border country. The rolling landscape of hills, forests, river valleys and ruined abbeys was his ancestral home, and throughout his expedition he sought out, listened to and wrote down the local poetry and ballads. These oral accounts, which he first heard as a young boy, had been passed down from generation to generation, and told of centuries of war between Lowlanders and the English, and the exploits, rivalries and blood feuds of reivers, brigands and clansmen. In 1802, the anthology was published as *The Minstrelsy of the Scottish Border*, and was soon on its way to becoming a sensation. The original print run sold out within six months in Scotland and England; it was translated into German, Danish and Swedish; and an American edition gave its author a first taste of transatlantic fame.

By this time the lawyer, whose name was Walter Scott, had been appointed Sheriff of Selkirkshire. And his *Minstrelsy* was just the start of one of the most influential careers in the history of English literature. Over the next three decades, Scott would 'invent' the historical novel and – for a time – become the most famous and successful writer in the world. What made his poems and novels unique was that he put his romantic heroes at the centre of genuine, immaculately researched historical events, all set in a real Scottish landscape described with unerring accuracy and a painterly eye for detail. By investing the nation's past with a mystical appeal, he also placed in the imagination of his readers a new appreciation of its landscapes. The American author Washington Irving was underwhelmed when first shown the Borders country by Scott, but soon came to revise his opinion, admitting that, 'such had been the magic web … thrown over the whole that it had greater charm for me than the richest scenery I had beheld'. The unabashed aim of Scott's work was to ensure the preservation of Scottish identity – creating powerful emotional touchstones during a period of unprecedented upheaval. As he himself wrote, 'What makes Scotland Scotland is fast disappearing'.

From the mid eighteenth century onwards, the nation's political, philosophical, economic – and physical – landscapes had been undergoing revolutionary change. Nowhere was this more pronounced than in the Lowlands. A new intellectual elite, largely based in Edinburgh, had set about tackling the challenge of transforming Scotland into a rational, efficient and – above all – modern nation. From the philosopher David Hume to the pioneering economist Adam Smith, Scotland suddenly found itself as a world leader in progressive thought.

This Scottish Enlightenment had such impact because its ideas were intensely practical in nature. Agriculture in particular fascinated the theorists. The landowner and legal philosopher Lord Kames dubbed it the 'chief of the arts', and was one of a number who advocated a new, rational approach – one that would alter fundamentally the relationship between man and his environment. Rather than accepting the landscape as a gift of nature, it was proposed that it could be altered for the better – or 'improved' – by wholesale, systematic intervention. As a result, from the mid eighteenth century onwards, the old order of the Lowlands was wiped clean away. Gone were the organic sprawl of fields and the meandering strips of rig and furrow. And in their place came a vast, ordered, geometric grid, separated by the straight lines of stone walls, roads and hedges – the unmistakable signature of the modern age.

The landowners presiding over these sweeping changes were eager to demonstrate their new status as masters of an 'Enlightened' landscape. Social standing was defined increasingly by the display of material status, and the country estate became the ultimate symbol of taste and refinement. Here, landscapes were created within landscapes. Planned 'wildernesses' – with deliberately informal yet still intricately designed walks and gardens – were manufactured as counterpoints to the newly enclosed and regulated countryside. Driving the fashion for the grand mansions built at the heart of these estates was the pre-eminent Scottish architectural dynasty of the eighteenth century: the Adam family. Following on from their influential father William, sons Robert and James looked back to ancient Greece and Rome with their designs, yet at the same time they attempted to translate the elegance and beauty of antiquity into a modern idiom. Once again, the idea of 'improvement' was central to this philosophy – by drawing on the ancient standards they believed architecture itself could become a civilising instrument.

Walter Scott was born a child of the Scottish Enlightenment and was a product of the world defined by Adam Smith – the world of profit and the market. He had watched his nation take the great leap forward to modernity, but in his heart he felt something was being lost forever. His romantic and inspirational view of Scotland's past established a tourist and nostalgia industry that remains central to the national economy to this day. He created and defined the Scottish landscape – but his was a landscape of history and the imagination. Even as Scott sat at his writing desk, the physical environment around him was being altered forever. Commerce, business, agriculture and industry were carving up the Lowlands to the clear and distinctive blueprint of progress.

In the borderlands between the Highlands and Lowlands, the River Teith flows out from the Trossachs to pass the fourteenth century Doune Castle. In Walter Scott's first novel, *Waverley*, set during the 1745 Rebellion, the eponymous hero is taken to the castle – at that time a Jacobite stronghold: 'on the opposite banks of the river, and partly surrounded by a winding of its stream, stood a large and massive castle, the half-ruined turrets of which were already glittering in the first rays of the sun … Upon one of these a sentinel watched, whose bonnet and plaid, streaming in the wind, declared him to be a Highlander'. Here was Scott's groundbreaking technique of placing his heroes within the basic context of historical fact. As Waverley approached the castle, the author noted that, 'The country around was at once fertile and romantic. Steep banks of wood were broken by cornfields, which this year presented an abundant harvest'. Today, Doune Castle sits within some of the nation's most 'improved' and intensively cultivated farmland.
DP084439 2009

Thought to have been a royal hunting lodge from as early as the eleventh century, the estate at Glamis has gone through many incarnations – from medieval castle to sixteenth century royal residence, Scottish Baronial house to baroque palace, and finally to great Victorian pile. The landscape of Glamis today is a mixture of the informal and the formal, with deliberately scattered plantations of trees cut through by the long line of an entrance avenue.
DP097011 2010

LEFT

At the northern fringes of the Lammermuir
hills in East Lothian, low sunlight casts
deep shadows from the remains of the
hillfort of White Castle. Built overlooking
the Thorter Burn – believed to be the route
of an ancient trackway from the southern
uplands to the coast – White Castle was
one of a number of similar structures
that studded the rounded summits of
the surrounding landscape some 2,500
years ago. From the top of its substantial
triple ramparts, the view northwards takes
in the volcanic plugs of Traprain Law and
Berwick Law, both also sites of prominent
hillforts during the Iron Age.

DP049803 2008

ABOVE

On the eastern fringes of the Moorfoot
Hills, between Peebles and Penicuik,
the Northshield Rings sit on a low hilltop,
partly hidden by plantation trees. As at
White Castle, here the low light picks
out the rampart remains.

DP037771 2007

LEFT

A flight above the Borders and the southern uplands reveals a vista of rounded hills plunging steeply to winding river valleys. With summits blanketed by snow, the remains of earth and stone ramparts – fragments left behind by an extensive network of hillforts – become obvious symbols in the landscape. These remarkable survival patterns of Iron Age settlement proliferate to the south of the Forth and in the Tweed Basin. Here overlooking the Scottish–English border to the east of Kelso, the hillfort of Green Humbleton crowns a summit with double lines of stone walling.

DP085004 2010

TOP RIGHT

The term 'hillfort' can be misleading, as it suggests a predominantly defensive structure built during times of war. Archaeologists believe, however, that conflict was rarely the reason behind their construction, and that they were places to live – villages enclosed by walls and wooden stockades, their elevated positions indicating ownership over surrounding farmlands. At Whiteside Hill to the north-west of Peebles, this fort looks out over the fertile valley of the Lyne Water, a tributary of the River Tweed.

DP085932 2010

BOTTOM RIGHT

At Orchard Rig to the south of the Cardrona Forest in the Tweed valley, the remains of house platforms fill the interior of the enclosure.

DP086082 2010

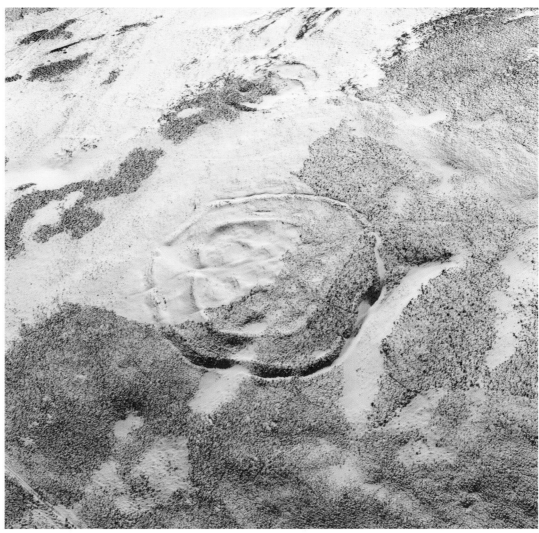

On the highest of the three summits towering over the lower Tweed valley are the remains of one of the largest hillforts in Scotland. Eildon Hill North is encircled by over three miles of ramparts enclosing a huge area of around 40 acres. First built around 3,000 years ago, the fort developed and evolved over time, with archaeologists discovering the remains of at least 300 wooden huts within its borders. Given the size of the hillfort – and its prominent position on the largest of the Eildons – many experts believe that the purpose of this structure could not have been defensive, and that it was built as an awe-inspiring venue for some important political or religious ritual. In the first century AD, the Romans established the massive military camp of Trimontium – named after the three Eildons – in the shadow of the northern hill, and then erected a solitary watchtower on the summit, amid the ruins of the abandoned fort. With vistas stretching tens of miles in every direction, this would have been a key position for sending and receiving signals, and for monitoring the movement of people across the landscape.

DP026872 2007

In the famous early-Victorian guidebook *Black's Picturesque Tourist of Scotland*, the ruined remains of Castle Campbell are described with a flourish as, 'occupying a wild and romantic situation on the top of a high and almost insulated rock … The mount on which it is situated is neatly encompassed on all sides by thick bosky woods, and mountain rivulets descending on either side unite at the base. Immediately behind rises a vast amphitheatre of wooded hills.' Certainly, the drama of the location is difficult to ignore. Situated above the town of Dollar in the southern fringes of the Ochil Hills, the Castle is hemmed-in by the ravines of the Burn of Care and the Burn of Sorrow, and, when first built in the early fifteenth century, was known rather mournfully as 'Castle Glume'. Just like ancient hillforts, castles were not always structures built for war, defence or conquest. The powerful Highland clan chief Colin Campbell, first Earl of Argyll, acquired the property around 1465, and saw in it the potential to create a Lowland *pied à terre* close to the royal court at Stirling. In 1493 an Act of Parliament granted the Earl the right to rename 'Castle Glume' as 'Campbell', and the building was renovated as a potent status symbol and place for entertaining the senior nobility – John Knox and James VI were both guests here, as was Mary Queen of Scots, who attended the wedding of the sister of the sixth Earl in January 1563. The Castle also excited the imagination of Walter Scott – in his Scottish history *Tales of a Grandfather*, he recounted how civil war in the seventeenth century 'doomed this magnificent pile to flames and ruin' at the hands of the Marquis of Montrose. For Scott, just as today, the 'majestic remains … still excite a sigh in those who view them'.

DP061734 2009

In the shadow of the red sandstone ruins of Edzell Castle, the 'great garden' is a symbol of how art can influence a landscape – an imprint of the seventeenth century European Renaissance in the heart of rural Angus. The Castle was the home of the Lindsay family from the mid fourteenth century, and it was David, the ninth Earl, who was responsible for the creation of the garden in 1604.

A space for intellectual contemplation, the garden was designed to stimulate the mind and senses, with wall carvings depicting planets, the cosmos and the heavens. Although the present garden is a recreation dating from the 1930s, the walled enclosure remains as a tantalising fragment of a burgeoning artistic and intellectual movement in Scotland.

DP097259 2010

In 1716, John Dalrymple – the second Earl of Stair and the British ambassador to Paris – returned to his home of Castle Kennedy to be confronted by a burnt-out ruin. Reputedly his domestic staff had set alight his bedding by airing it too close to an open fire, and the blaze had spread to consume the mansion house. Unbowed by this disaster, Dalrymple and his chief gardener Thomas McCalla embarked on a lavish reconstruction of the surrounding landscape. The ruins, set on a narrow isthmus between the White and Black Lochs, became a 'picturesque' centrepiece for some 70 acres of gardens. The result was a masterpiece of classical eighteenth century landscaping – a complex array of woodland avenues and rides filled with exotic plants. By 1733, Castle Kennedy was a recognised place to visit, and a year later the poet Samuel Boyse captured the essence of the gardens, describing them as 'Too form'd for Nature – yet too wild for Art'. In 1864, 150 years after the fire, the Stair family built Lochinch Castle – a new residence on the estate situated overlooking Dalrymple's garden landscape.

ABOVE **DP052050** 2008
FOLLOWING PAGES **DP052060** 2008

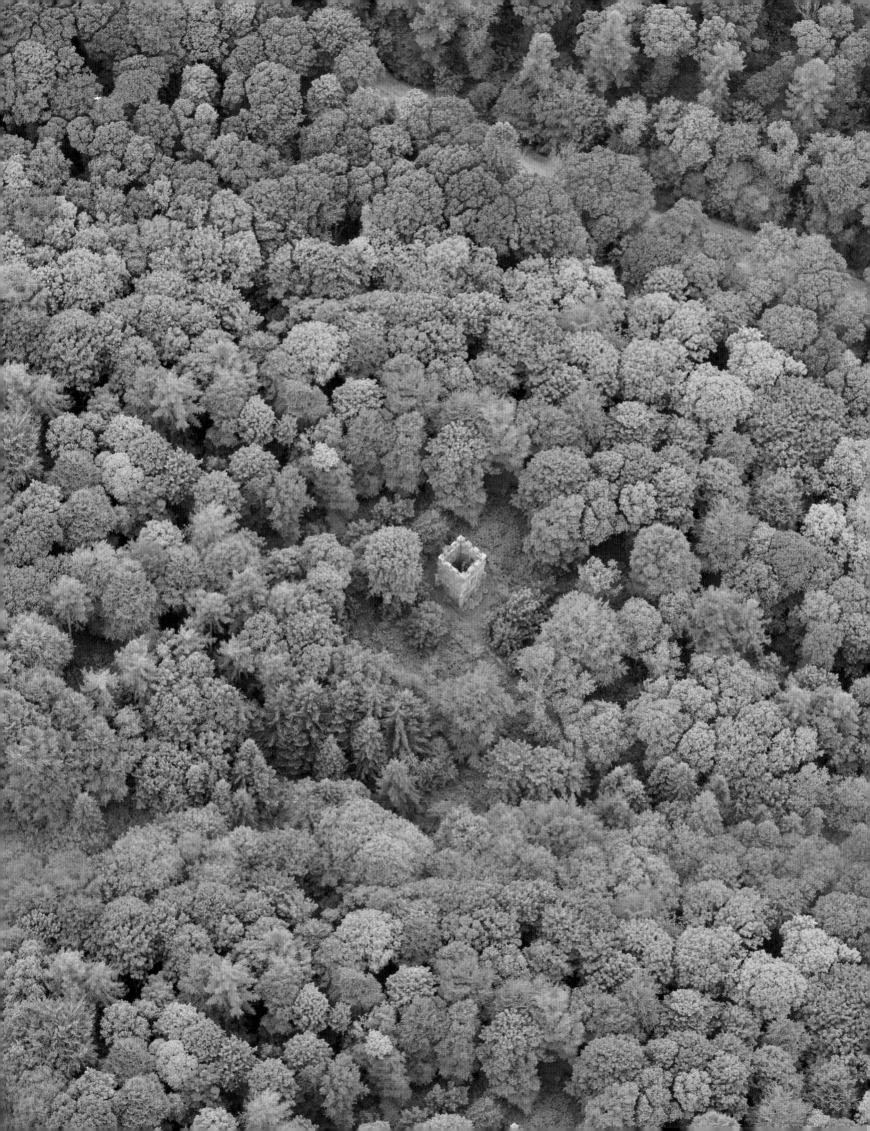

In a small clearing surrounded by dense woodland stands the 'Temple' – a folly built purely for decoration amid the estate of Cally House to the south of Gatehouse of Fleet. The renowned landscape gardener James Ramsay constructed the gothic Temple in 1779, on a rise of land that allowed it to be seen by travellers on the road linking Gatehouse to Girthon.

This was just one feature in a landscape intended to advertise taste and status. In the late eighteenth century, the then owner James Murray tried to create the illusion of an ancient medieval park stocked with game – even importing fallow deer and white cattle from Cadzow, and allowing them to roam free as part of a 'wild' idyll. DP070799 2009

In the late eighteenth and early nineteenth centuries, Thomas White and the renowned architect James Playfair redesigned Raith Park as an ambitious picturesque landscape. The Raith Tower, pictured here rising above a thicket of trees on the high ground of Comrie Hill, was one of several follies constructed as eyecatchers on the outer fringes of the estate. DP042474 2008

In 1753, the author Daniel Defoe visited Kinross House on the banks of Loch Leven, and was enchanted by what he saw: 'At the west end of the Lake – the gardens reaching down to the very water's edge – stands the most beautiful and regular piece of architecture in all of Scotland.' Situated on a peninsula on the western shore of the Loch, with panoramic views to the Lomond Hills in the east and Glendevon Forest to the west, the whole house and its gardens were deliberately tied in to the surrounding landscape. Kinross was the work of Sir William Bruce, Charles II's 'Surveyor General of the Royal Works' in Scotland, and the pre-eminent Scottish architect of the late seventeenth and early eighteenth centuries. As with his house at Balcaskie – where Bruce focused his gardens on the natural feature of the Bass Rock – here he recast Loch Leven Castle, the former island prison of Mary Queen of Scots, as a ruined folly. Such was his attention to detail that he even had one of the Castle's turrets partially repaired to improve the 'picturesque' quality of the view from the House. Kinross was Bruce's masterpiece, a triumph of design that re-imagined the landscape and the surroundings as a work of art.

DP086882 2010

LEFT

Set in a broad river valley to the north of Strathblane, Duntreath Castle has been in the possession of the Edmonstones since the fifteenth century. In the nineteenth century, Sir Archibald Edmonstone transformed the castle into a Franco-Scots palace, and by the Edwardian era the exuberance of its architecture and the magnificence of its interiors saw it become a play-park for high society. As the twentieth century progressed, the scale and opulence of the house made it unmanageable, and in 1958 extensive demolitions were carried out – leaving behind the towerhouse, house and gatehouse that we see today.

DP049053 2008

RIGHT

Amid the rolling hills of the Southern Uplands, Drumlanrig Castle is one of the finest designed landscapes in Scotland. The original seventeenth century layout of the castle and its gardens is believed to have been influenced by Sir William Bruce, and alterations over the centuries involved noted designers and Enlightenment figures including the third Duke of Queensberry, architect William Burn, and even Walter Scott. In 1856, the First Edition of the Ordnance Survey Map of Scotland recorded 80 miles of scenic pathways weaving through Drumlanrig's sprawling landscape.

DP104033 2010

Set above the banks of the – reputedly man-made – Lochnaw Loch in the Rhins of Galloway, Lochnaw Castle is the ancestral seat of the Agnews, the one-time hereditary sheriffs of the region.

The castle's four-storey towerhouse dates from the sixteenth century, although subsequent extensions to the building, and an adjacent mansion built in the Victorian era, have since been demolished.

DP105895 2010

One of the most unusual features of
Lochnaw Castle is its large, hexagonal
walled garden. Reached by paths running
through a dense forest plantation, the
garden today encloses one of the most
diverse collections of fruit trees in Britain.

DP105894 2010

In the eighteenth century, when William Roy produced his 'Military Maps', he recorded Kinnaird Castle surrounded by parkland – a design that may have been the work of William Bruce. The ancestral home of the Carnegie family since 1402, Kinnaird evolved as a product of fashion and mixed fortunes. After the 1715 Rebellion, the fifth Earl was exiled for his support of the Jacobites, and the estates went to seed.

Kinnaird's resurrection came during the Enlightenment, when James Playfair rebuilt the house, and Thomas White recast the landscape as a planned wilderness. From 1885, Kinnaird was remodelled by David Bryce, and the estate grew to 22,500 acres – an extraordinary example of a landscape manufactured within a landscape.

LEFT DP097180 2010

ABOVE DP097196 2010

While some designed landscapes remain preserved across the centuries – or have been recovered and restored – others are less fortunate. In the valley of the River North Esk, on the urban fringes of Edinburgh, Mavisbank is a derelict and desolate remnant of a former glory.

The estate's classical villa was designed in a collaboration between the two leading architectural figures of the early eighteenth century: William Adam and Sir John Clerk of Penicuik. As well as co-designer of Mavisbank, Clerk was also its owner, and wanted the house as a residence to allow him to manage more closely his coal workings at nearby Loanhead.

DP033501 2007

Over the course of the eighteenth and nineteenth centuries, Mavisbank changed hands on a number of occasions, and in 1876 it was converted into a private mental institution. In 1973 a major fire gutted the house, and Mavisbank has been abandoned ever since.

While debate goes on as to the future of the property – which is one of the most important in the architectural history of Scotland – the house and its designed estates have become a picture of decay, set within a surrounding Lowland landscape changed forever by coal-mining and heavy industry.

DP033498 2007

Since the beginning of the industrial revolution, the search for mineral energy has had a dramatic impact on the appearance of the landscapes of lowland Scotland. Near Muirkirk in East Ayshire, the opencast workings of the Viaduct Mine have carved a hillside apart, as the rock itself becomes a resource to be scoured and processed for coal. Only a few kilometres away, the Common Hill windfarm seeks to provide an alternative form of energy – renewable power generated by the spin of its turbines.

DP087004 2009

In golden, late-summer sunlight, the great sweep of the Almond Valley Railway Viaduct cuts through harvest fields between Broxburn and Newbridge. Designed by the engineer John Miller for a high-speed line between Edinburgh and Glasgow, this massive Victorian viaduct was opened in 1842 and is made up of 36 ashlar-faced arches, each of 50ft span, with some reaching up to 70ft in height.

As the central Lowlands were rapidly transformed into the industrial heartland of Scotland in the nineteenth century, thousands of miles of iron rails forged out across a landscape that had once been dominated only by agriculture.

DP095389 2010

The M74 motorway cuts through the low hills of Wedder Law on its way to the sprawling outskirts of Glasgow. Invisible to those on the road, the remains of a lost industrial landscape emerge when viewed from above.

This empty stretch of moorland was once the site of a complex of lime quarries, with a series of kilns built alongside to heat the stone and transform it in to quicklime.
DP086986 2009

FOLLOWING PAGES
Above the village of Newburgh on the banks of the Firth of Tay, the Clatchard Craig Quarry has taken a huge bite out of the side of Ormiston Hill, exposing its rocky interior.
DP111480 2011

Just inland from the Links of Machrihanish
on the Mull of Kintrye, the field systems
of Balnagleck Farm lay a series of ordered
geometric panels over the landscape.
From above it becomes clear just how
remorselessly the 'improvement' farms
divided up the landscape of the past –
here, the remains of walling and strips
of rig and furrow are sliced apart by

the lines of the modern fields. Picked out
in shadow at the top corner of the end field
are remains dating even further back –
a 2,000-year-old drystone structure
known as a 'Dun', now enclosed by
ruler-straight field walls.

DP056806 2008

Just to the north of the Solway Firth
in Dumfries and Galloway, a farming
patchwork spreads out to the horizon.
From the mid eighteenth century onwards,
this was the modern blueprint that erased
the old landscape of the Lowlands.

DP052279 2008

The fertile carselands of the Firth of Forth, which stretch some 50 miles from the Lake of Menteith, through Stirling, to Grangemouth, are a remarkable landscape archive of environmental change and human activity. Bounded to the north by the fault scarp of the Ochil Hills, this whole area was inundated by the sea some 9,000 years ago, after the end of the last Ice Age. Raised volcanic plugs – like Stirling's castle

rock, pictured top left – were islands in a vast estuary that, at high tide, covered an area 25km long by 6km wide. Around 7,000 years ago the waters receded, and the carse began to be covered in oak woodland and raised peat bog. From the mid eighteenth century onwards, this floodplain was a focal point for the agricultural 'improvers', as the massive peat deposits – sometimes 6 metres thick – were cleared to reach the

fertile earth beneath. The Enlightenment farmer-philosopher Lord Kames was a key figure in this initiative, leasing out his lands on the carse on the condition that tenants – so-called 'moss-lairds' – first stripped the peat and then floated it off down the Forth. In the process, remarkable fragments of the landscape's history were revealed, including the skeletons of at least 15 whales – some up to 21m long – that may have been stranded

thousands of years before on the mudflats of the estuary. Stone tools found alongside the remains suggest that our ancestors stripped the carcasses for meat. Today, the carse is one of the most fertile, productive – and 'improved' – agricultural landscapes in Scotland.

TOP LEFT DP079016 2010
BOTTOM LEFT DP079015 2010
ABOVE DP075286 2010

Fragmenting ice-sheets concertina
towards the head of the Talla Dam near
Tweedsmuir in the Scottish Borders.
In the late nineteenth century, survey
engineers for the Edinburgh and District
Water Trust identified Talla as an ideal site
for a new reservoir to supply the increasing
water demands of the city. Construction
began in 1895, and involved extending
the Caledonian Railway from Broughton
to the newly built terminus of 'Victoria
Lodge', just below the works. The dam itself
was built around a core of over 100,000
tons of clay brought in from Carluke in
Lanarkshire. Once material arrived at
the Lodge, it was shipped to the site by
means of a 'Blondin' – an overhead
ropeway named after the famous
Frenchman Charles Blondin, who crossed
Niagara Falls on a tightrope in 1859.
In addition to the dam, the scheme also
required a 28-mile-long aqueduct system
to transfer the millions of gallons of
water to Edinburgh. This included the
construction of the Tweed Viaduct,
a 100-ft girder bridge which carried the
railway and the pipeline over the river at
Glenrusco. The official opening ceremony
was carried out on 25 September 1905
with dignitaries travelling by rail from
Edinburgh. *The Scotsman* reported on
the ceremony the following day: 'To many,
this part of the country, hitherto somewhat
inaccessible, was quite new, and the view
of the infant Tweed and high hill screen of
the valley in its beautiful autumn colouring
was very much enjoyed. The scene at the
reservoir had quite a gala day aspect.
The roadway to the embankment and
the great dam across the valley were set
off by lines of streamers. The Victoria villa
was decorated with festoons of crimson
cloth and shields … at the head of which
was the Scottish Lion on its field of gold'.

DP085982 2010

Just a few miles to the east of Loch Talla, the Megget Reservoir is contained by the largest earth dam ever constructed in Scotland. The scheme was first considered in 1963 in order to supply more fresh water to meet demand in Edinburgh and the Lothians – although construction did not begin until 1976.

The valley of Megget had been farmed for centuries – and included the remains of a tower-house used by Mary Queen of Scots and James VI as a hunting lodge – and in the 1970s was still home to a community of farmers and shepherds, with roads, farm buildings, a school and a church. By the time of the dam's completion in 1983, this entire landscape was submerged under 64 million tonnes of water.

Interviewed at the time of construction, the valley's former schoolmistress said, 'At first I thought it was just the end of everything. And then I began to think it would be wonderful if Megget valley can provide life for thousands of people, and it will be very beautiful.'
DP049345 2008

A lone tractor kicks up a great trail of dust in a field at Knockgerran in South Ayshire. Above the farm and spreading out past the Penwhapple Reservoir is the Hadyard Hill Windfarm, a cluster of 52 turbines all standing at least 60m in height.

DP106466 2011

ABOVE

Surrounded by freshly-ploughed fields, Brechin Golf Course fans out on either side of the A90 dual carriageway in the flatlands of the Montrose Basin. With over 550 golf courses in Scotland, large tracts of the modern landscape have been distinctively shaped for the pursuit of leisure.

In the Lowlands, courses show up as manicured patchworks – lush green parklands enclosed by trees, dotted with sand traps, and stretching out among arable fields.

DP111582 2011

RIGHT

Golf courses are often designed to use the natural contours of the landscape. Here at Bishop Hill on the eastern banks of Loch Leven, the nine-hole, heathland golf course of Bishopshire merges into the steep, sandstone slopes above the small village of Kinesswood.

DP111466 2011

Directly below the crags of Stirling Castle are the most remarkable remains of any garden in Scotland. Known as the 'King's Knot', this geometric pattern of earthworks is thought to date from the early sixteenth century, although its exact origins remain unclear. As a result, a considerable mythology has grown up around the site. Medieval tradition associated Stirling with the legends of King Arthur, and in the fourteenth century the Scottish poet John Barbour wrote of how the park of Stirling Castle was 'close by the Round Table'. Recent archaeological surveys have done little to dispel the myth, uncovering the remains of an earlier circular feature directly beneath the King's Knot. The idea that the royal park was the site where Arthur and his knights held counsel is a potent one, and may explain both the persistence of the associations and the unusual design of the garden. Arthurian Legend was a feature of the entertainments of the Stewart kings at Stirling Castle, and James IV even named his son and heir – who died in infancy – Arthur. It is possible that the King's Knot was constructed as an elaborate landscape tribute to the myth.

LEFT DP114711 1992

RIGHT SC1018862 1992

Heavy industry has transformed the Lowlands of Scotland over the past two hundred years. Many landscapes have come and gone, leaving behind the debris of collieries, giant oil-shale bings, flooded quarries and overgrown railway lines. This is the archaeology of the industrial revolution – poignant reminders of a time when Scotland was the engine room of the British Empire. But not all of these landscapes are abandoned once their mineral worth is exhausted. At St Ninian's Opencast Mine to the north of Dunfermline – where over 5 million tons of coal have been extracted in the last decade – a project is transforming the great tear of the mine-works into a vast piece of art. The renowned American landscape architect Charles Jencks is using the heaped 'overburden' earth mounds from the coaling operations – as pictured here – to create the 'Scottish World Project': a sculpted, abstract parkland representing the continents of the world, and centred on a loch carved into the shape of Scotland.

DP110947 2011

1 Doune Castle, Stirling

2 Glamis Castle, Angus

3 White Castle, East Lothian

4 The Northshield Rings, Eddleston

5 Green Humbleton, Kelso

6 Whiteside Hill, Tweeddale

7 Orchard Rig, Tweeddale

8 Eildon Hills, Melrose

9 Castle Campbell, Dollar

10 Edzell Walled Garden, Angus

11 Castle Kennedy, Dumfries and Galloway

11 Castle Kennedy, Dumfries and Galloway

12 The 'Temple', Cally House, Gatehouse of Fleet

13 The Raith Tower, Comrie Hill

14 Kinross House, Loch Leven

15 Duntreath Castle, Strathblane

16 Drumlanrig Castle, Dumfries and Galloway

17 Lochnaw Castle, Rhins of Galloway

17 Lochnaw Castle, Rhins of Galloway

18 Kinnaird Castle, Montrose

18 Kinnaird Castle, Montrose

19 Mavisbank House, Loanhead

19 Mavisbank House, Loanhead

20 Viaduct Opencast Mine, Muirkirk

21 Almond Valley Railway Viaduct, Newbridge

22 M74 motorway, Wedder Law

23 Clatchard Craig Quarry, Newburgh, Firth of Tay

24 Balnagleck Farm, Mull of Kintrye

25 Dalton, Dumfries and Galloway

26 The Carse of Forth, Stirling

26 The Carse of Forth, Stirling

27 The Carse of Forth, Grangemouth

28 Talla Dam, Tweedsmuir

29 Megget Reservoir, Tweedsmuir

30 Hadyard Hill Wind Farm, Knockgerran

31 Brechin Golf Course, Angus

32 Bishopshire Golf Course, Bishop Hill, Loch Leven

33 The King's Knot, Stirling Castle

33 The King's Knot, Stirling Castle

34 The Scottish World Project, St Ninian's Opencast Mine, Dunfermline

Lowlands Locations

Aerial reconnaissance across all of Scotland's landscapes has shown itself to be one of the most effective forms of archaeological survey. Not only does it provide fresh perspectives on known sites, it is also responsible for locating and identifying many thousands of previously undiscovered structures and remains. There is a sense of acute anticipation before every flight – a feeling that, by gazing down at the complex patterns of human intervention left in the landscape, new, nationally important sites could be found at any time.

Perhaps the surveyor will spot the circular stone walls of an ancient fortification crowning a rounded hilltop, or the crop marks of a previously unknown Roman camp emerging in a farmer's field. Either way, the thrill of the chase and the adrenaline rush of discovery remain just as potent, even at the end of a long day of flying.

• INVERNESS

• ABERDEEN

10
31
18
2

23
14 32
9
1 26 13
33 27 34
15
21• EDINBURGH
• GLASGOW 19 3
4
6
7 8
5
20 22 28 29
24
30
16
25
17
11 12

Coastlines

Sometime around the tenth century AD, on the Ardnamurchan peninsula in the western Highlands, a group of Vikings dragged a boat inland from a sheltered beach. This was no ordinary coastal landing, however. As they reached a low mound above the shore, they began to dig a hole in the earth about 5 metres long and 1.5 metres wide. After manoeuvring the boat into this channel, they then lowered the body of a dead warrior carefully down into its wooden hull. Once in position, they arranged a host of possessions around the body. A shield was placed over the chest, while a spear, axe and an iron sword – with a beautifully decorated silver pommel and a bone hilt – were laid alongside. They also added a bronze drinking horn, flints for making fire, a metal pan, pottery from the Hebrides, a bronze ring-pin from Ireland, and a whetstone from Norway. Finally, the boat was filled almost completely with rocks. This burial ritual was reserved only for Vikings of the highest status: for chieftains, or great, ocean-going adventurers. The boat itself was a symbol of a life connected intimately to the sea. It is surely no coincidence that this final resting place looks out past the island of Eigg and the rocky peaks of Rum to where the sun sets on the open water.

The Ardnamurchan Viking remained lost for over 1,000 years, until the grave was chanced upon in 2011 by a team of archaeologists working on the peninsula. Believing at first that the burial mound was debris deposited by farmers during field clearances, closer inspection revealed hundreds of metal rivets – many attached to rotten slivers of wood – laid out in the distinctive outline of the pointed prow and stern of a Viking boat. Fragments of an arm bone and several teeth were all that were left of the warrior. But, along with the possessions and the wooden remains, archaeologists believe that laboratory testing may reveal where this person came from, and even the origin of the trees felled to build their vessel.

This discovery, thought to be the first complete Viking ship burial found on the British mainland, would be remarkable enough on its own. But it is in fact just one of a number of monuments to the dead left in this bay going back almost 6,000 years. On a hillock just above the Norse burial site there is a stone cairn built around 4000 BC, with an internal chamber where human remains were placed. Over time the way people were buried in this cairn changed, from cremations to tight bundles of bones, and then, a thousand or more years after it was first constructed, a single, complete body was laid to rest along with pieces of pottery. This last burial saw the cairn sealed for good. Yet about 1800 BC, and just 10 metres away, a new tomb was built.

Again, a single body was placed inside, this time with a jet bead necklace –
a sign of far-flung trading connections – before the entrance to the grave
was blocked off. There was clearly something special about this place,
something that, over an extraordinarily long period of time, brought
different people and cultures to the same spot to commemorate their dead.

For millennia the coast has been a gateway for the people of Scotland –
landing ground for hunter-gatherers; beachhead for Viking raiders; staging
point to strike out to abundant fishing grounds; borderland to the open
highway of the sea. With so many lives half-lived on the water, it seems no
surprise that communities would view the coastline as a symbolic location
for ritual and remembrance. Perhaps these monument-graves were placed
deliberately on the 'edge', in a landscape part-earth, part-sea; a landscape
that defined the traditions and myths of the people who lived there –
and also of those who were just passing through.

Of course, not all remains are designed to be lasting memorials, and there
is more to this one Ardnamurchan bay than just ancient tombs. Immediately
to the west of the beach, on a rocky promontory overlooking the inlet, there
is evidence of a fort dating back to about 200 BC, with traces of burning and
slag that hint at a centre for Iron Age metalworking. A thousand years before
the Vikings arrived to perform their burial ritual, it is clear that there was a
strategic need to watch the seas and mark ownership of the surrounding land.
And it does not end there. Close to the fort, on a crescent of hillside, there are
the rocky footings left behind by a nineteenth century farming community.
The people of this township had worked the land of the bay up until 1853 –
and then their houses were abandoned and demolished to make way for a
sheep pasture.

This is just one tiny fragment of Scotland's near 12,000km of coastline,
a sliver of land on a Highland peninsula now seen as remote to our modern
eyes. Yet its long, varied history demonstrates the cultural richness of our
coastal landscape, and the enduring importance of the sea. Take almost any
beach, bay, dune or cliff-side, and you will find the layered traces of man's
presence across time, from ancient harbours, promontory castles and
medieval saltpans to stone 'fish-traps' and smugglers' caves. The shoreline
has represented security, survival, opportunity and adventure over many
thousands of years. Yet a day does not go by without the inexorable shift
of this physical border. From the coming and going of the tides, to rising
sea levels and the never-ending process of erosion, the histories and
memories contained within this landscape are at once enduringly
vibrant and dangerously fragile.

PREVIOUS PAGES
Behind the small nineteenth century
settlement of Sanna on the western tip of
the Ardnamurchan peninsula, a vast crater
of rock tells a story of the landscape going
back some 60 million years. As the North
Atlantic trench widened and the earth's
crust thinned, a line of volcanoes burst into
the western seaboard of Scotland, running
from St Kilda, Skye and Rum to Mull,
Arran and Ailsa Craig. At Ardnamurchan,
rings of once molten magma now define
a series of concentric circles – known as
a 'caldera' – which mark out the magma
chamber and foundations of a giant
volcano. The legacy of this turbulent
geological past is a fertile landscape –
today a farm even sits right in the centre
of the ancient volcano – and a coastline
of sheltered bays and rocky inlets that
has seen thousands of years of human
activity, from Neolithic and Viking burials
to medieval castles and crofting townships.
DP077090 2009

RIGHT
At Garmouth, the wide braided channel of
the River Spey flows into the Moray Firth.
This was once a key port for the timber
trade, receiving huge quantities of felled
trees floated down the river from the
forests of Glenmore, Abernethy and
Rothiemurchus. Shipyards and sawmills
sprang up along the coast, and the nearby
village of Kingston was established in
1784 by the Hull shipbuilding company
of Dodsworth and Osborne. In 1886,
a 368 ft-long viaduct built by the
Great North of Scotland Railway
bridged the wandering course of
the Spey. Although the line closed
in 1968, the viaduct remains in use
as a public footpath.
DP075571 2009

LEFT

Surrounded by steep slopes of clay and grass, the tidal inlet of Cove Harbour on the Borders coast has a history as a seaport dating back to the beginning of the seventeenth century. In 1744, Sir John Hall of Dunglass attempted to 'clear a basin' at Cove. Construction was 'considerably advanced' when a strong north-easterly wind raised a torrid sea and destroyed the works. A unique feature of this attempt at 'improvement' does remain however: a 56m-long tunnel, excavated using gunpowder, runs through the cliffs and is still the only way of accessing Cove at high tide. Today's sandstone piers, extending as pincers from the sweeping curves of natural rock, were built in 1831.

DP062437 2009

ABOVE

Originally known as Coldingham Shore, the Berwickshire village of St Abbs was developed in the 1830s by the Edinburgh brewing company 'Ushers' as a fishing station. The new name came from the Northumbrian Princess Ebbe, who founded a nunnery on a nearby promontory in the seventh century.

DP062470 2009

On a narrow peninsula projecting out into the Moray Firth, the ordered grid-iron layout of the village of Burghead is typical of the designed settlements of the early nineteenth century. Built between 1805 and 1809 as an industrial herring fishing station, Burghead has left the distinctive stamp of 'improvement' on the landscape. Yet the history of this promontory goes back much further. At the very tip of the headland are the earthwork remains of a once significant seat of power in the Pictish kingdom of northern Scotland. A massive fortification constructed here some 1,500 years ago was largely flattened by the linear rows of fishermen's cottages. However, a number of remarkable fragments of this site's history do still remain. Most unusual are the 'Burghead Bulls', a series of thirty bull carvings discovered during harbour construction works at the beginning of nineteenth century. Believed to be religious icons, territorial emblems or clan totems, the carvings are outstanding relics of Pictish art and culture – although today the whereabouts of only six of the original thirty are known, with the remaining stones held in both the National Museum of Scotland and the British Museum.

DP103344 2011

LEFT

On the tiny island of Eilean Loain near the head of Loch Sween, the thin arm of a jetty provides shelter and mooring for a private residence. To the south-west, where the long stretch of the loch meets the sea, is the twelfth century Castle Sween – thought to be one of the oldest surviving stone-built castles in Scotland.

DP108508 2011

ABOVE

Clustered around the perfect natural harbour of Loch a' Bhealiach on the western shore of Loch Sween, the village of Tayvallich – the name derived from the Gaelic meaning 'the house of the pass' – has been a key stopping-point for travellers for centuries. The old drovers roads once ran through the village, with black cattle from the Isle of Jura unloaded at Keills at the southern tip of the peninsula, and then taken onwards through Tayvallich to the markets at Falkirk and Stirling. Today the sheltered anchorage is a favourite of the yachting community, a perfect launch point to explore the coastline and islands of the western seaboard.

DP108507 2011

LEFT

The MV *Loch Dunvegan* car-ferry prepares
to leave the slipway at Rhubodach on the Isle
of Bute to make the short trip acros the Kyles
to the mainland terminal of Colintraive.

DP057317 2008

RIGHT

Beneath Sgurr Coire Choinnichan, the
whitewashed houses of Inverie Bay on
the Knoydart peninsula form the largest
settlement in mainland Britain not
connected to the road network. The only
way in or out of here has not changed for
millennia – involving either an arduous
walk over unforgiving terrain, or a journey
by sea. Once known as the 'Rough Bounds',
the landscape of Knoydart has a sometimes
violent, and often controversial history.
Passed from the Clan MacDonald to the
MacDonnells of Glengarry in the sixteenth
century, the estates were cleared to make
way for sheep farming in the nineteenth
century – with many of the 2,000 tenants
given free passage to start new lives in
Nova Scotia. Knoydart has changed hands
on several occasions since, spending much
of this time as a private sporting estate.
In 1999, however, the community raised
the funds to stage their own buyout, ending
centuries of feudal ownership. The 17,000
acres of 'Scotland's last wilderness' are now
the sole property of the people who call this
landscape their home.

DP110066 2011

On the far north coast of Scotland, the wide, sandy estuary of the Kyle of Tongue meets the sea. On the right is a tract of the landscape known as the Moine – Gaelic for 'Moor'. In the *Statistical Account of Sutherland*, written in the late eighteenth century, the Reverend William McKenzie and the Reverend Hugh Ross described how this, 'hilly desert, covered with dark heath, and interspersed with greyish rocks, impassable bogs, and stagnant pools of brownish water, presents a prospect uniformly rugged and dreary'. The pair were more taken, however, with the settlement of Tongue at the head of the Bay, recalling that 'an arm of the sea, skirted on each side with corn fields, enclosed pastures and farmhouses , stretches itself five miles into the land'. Most praise, however, was reserved for the mountain of Ben Hope, seen here on the far right: 'Its appearance, in a calm summer evening, when partly obscured by mist, is wonderfully grand, and infuses into the mind a sublime kind of melancholy'. The *Statistical Account* was the brainchild of Sir John Sinclair of Ulbster, MP for Caithness, whose plan was to ask ministers of the Church of Scotland throughout the country to reply to a set of planned questions on geography, climate, natural resources and social customs in their local parishes. Sir John's stated aim was to 'elucidate the Natural History and Political State of Scotland'. The returns from the parishes were compiled in a series of 21 volumes published between 1791 and 1799. These offer a fascinating picture of Scotland's landscapes at a time of rapid change – works of social and geographical accountancy that are a mixture of Enlightenment idealism and the often romantic prose of their Reverend authors.

DP093004 2010

LEFT

At the head of Luce Bay in the Rhins of Galloway, the Water of Luce runs past the Wigtownshire County Golf Course and exits into a shifting mosaic of sandbanks, reefs and sea. In the foreground, marked by a series of white breakers, is the shallow black 'V' of a 'fish trap' – a line of boulder walls embedded in the sand and designed to catch fish in the shallow waters of the river mouth.

DP095309 2010

RIGHT

The thin tendrils of the Lady Burn meander across the Baldoon Sands in Wigtown Bay in the far south-west of Scotland. The bay is the estuary of the Cree and Bladnoch Rivers, a wide expanse of intertidal mud flats, sand and salt marshes – known locally as the 'inks' – that forms Britain's largest Local Nature Reserve. This managed landscape is a unique wildlife environment in Scotland, providing an abundant habitat and feeding ground for everything from osprey and whooper swans to otters and rare fish like sparling and allis shad.

DP095343 2011

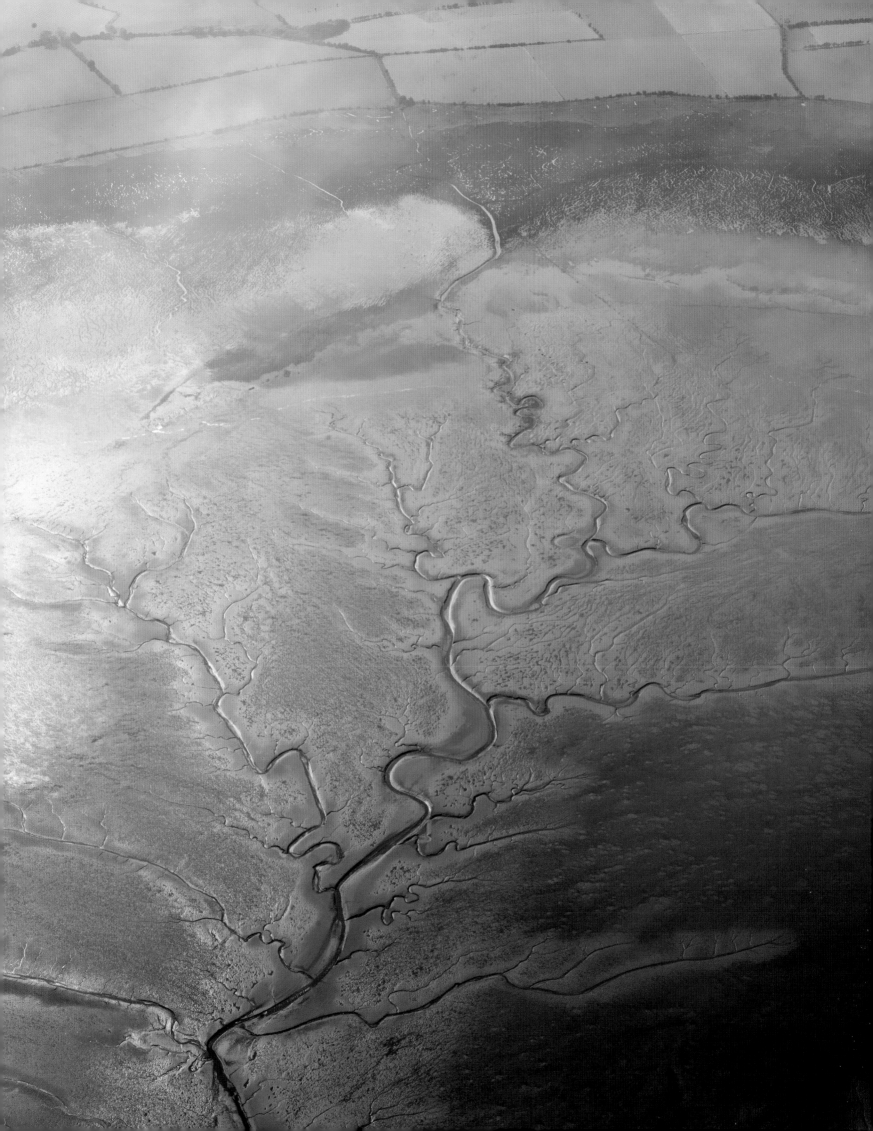

Facing out across the sea to Ireland, the
ruined shell of Dunskey Castle merges
into the rocky western coastline of the
Rhins of Galloway. First recorded as the
site of a castle in the fourteenth century,
the massive stone watch tower that looms
over the cliffs today was built by the Adairs
of Kinhilt at the beginning of the sixteenth
century. Hugh, first Viscount Montgomery,
extended the structure in 1620, yet by 1684,
in an account written by Andrew Symson,
the minister of nearby Kirkinner, Dunskey
is described as 'wholly ruinous'.

DP105871 2011

On the very edge of a sea cliff looking
out across the water to the Isle of Arran,
Greenan Castle is a four-storey towerhouse
built in 1603 by John Kennedy of Baltersan.
Abandoned in the eighteenth century,
the lonely ruins have provided inspiration
for artists and authors including Walter
Scott, who reputedly featured a fictionalised
version of Greenan in his short play

*The Doom of Devorgoil: An Ayrshire
Tragedy*, and George F Buchanan,
the nineteenth century landscape artist.
DP091139 2010

The roofless remains of Gylen Castle stand on the highest ridge of a rocky, arrowhead promontory at Kerrara in the western Highlands. The castle was built around 1582 as a stronghold for the Clan MacDougall, but was besieged and sacked just 60 years later by a Covenanter army under the command of General Leslie.

The ruins that remained provided dramatic evidence of Gylen's demise: fire-damaged stonework, carbonised roof timbers and floorboards, and singed bone. In the nineteenth century, the castle was seen as a wondrous fragment of a sublime landscape. In the romantic novel *Henrietta Temple*, published in 1837 by

the future Prime Minister Benjamin Disraeli, Gylen is described as 'The most picturesque object ... perched upon a wild promontory ... against which the sea has rolled in from the open Atlantic since ancient times ... The scene is one of savage and desolate grandeur.'

DP018035 2006

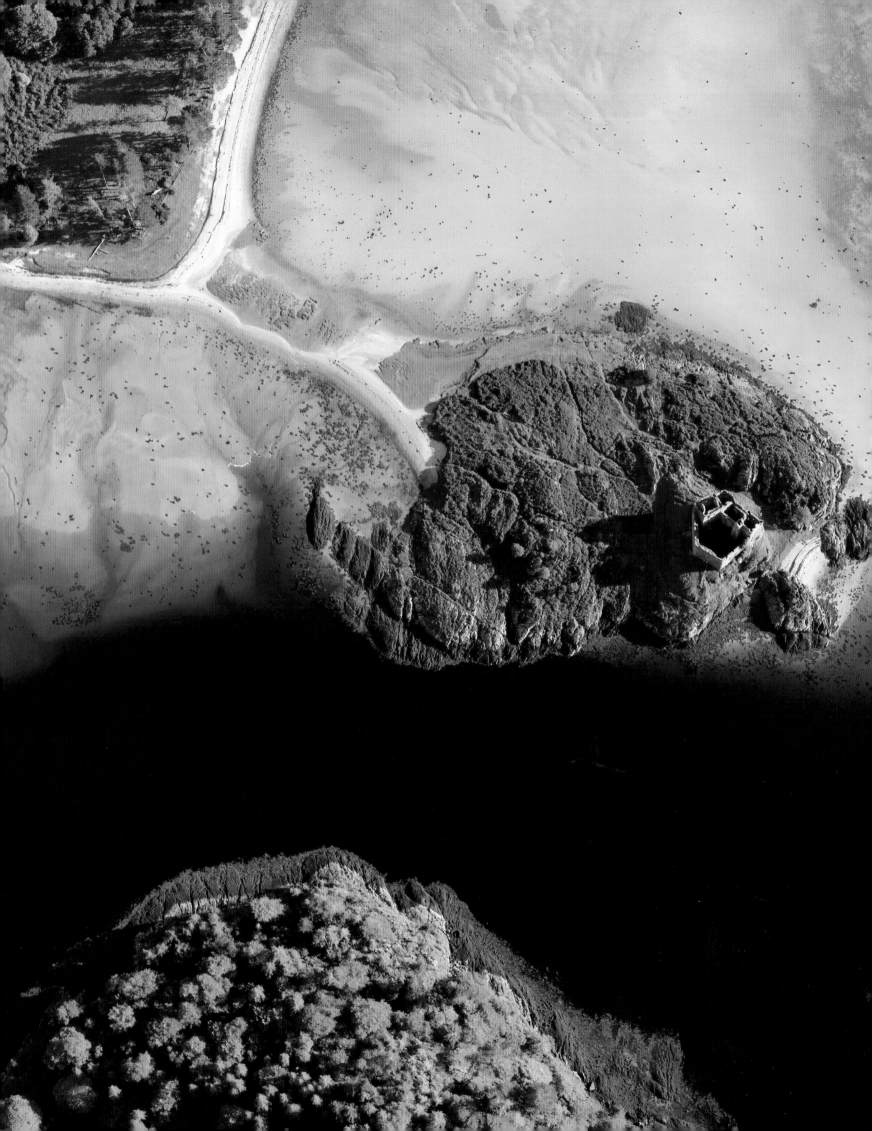

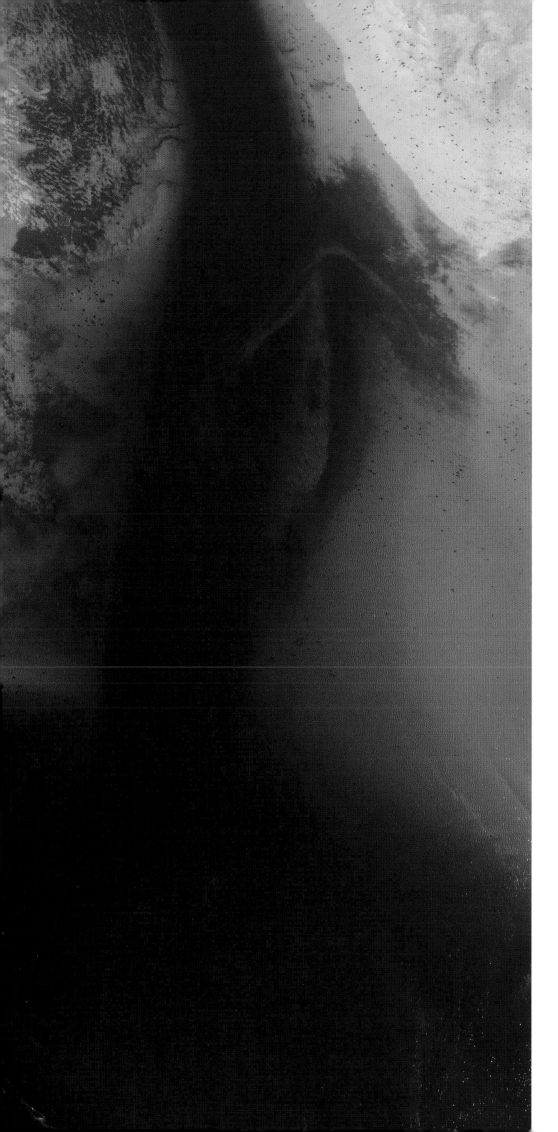

A castle has crowned the rocky outcrop of the tidal islet of Tioram – Gaelic for 'dry land' – at the mouth of Loch Moidart since the thirteenth century. The seat of the MacDonalds of Clanranald, the stronghold here was developed according to defensive necessity and architectural fashion over the course of five hundred years, until its abandonment in the eighteenth century. It was warfare that destroyed Tioram, but not directly. As the clan chief joined up with the forces of the Jacbobite Rebellion in 1715, he ordered that his own castle be destroyed to prevent it from falling into the hands of the Hanoverians. Over 40 years later, David Watson – a Scottish engineer and the Deputy Quarter-Master General of the Board of Ordnance – was one of the leading figures in the 'Military Survey' of the Highlands carried out in the wake of the 1745 Rebellion. In his notes taken on Tioram in 1748, assessing both its current state and potential strategic importance, Watson described the castle as, 'an old ruinous building belonging to the Clanranald family, it stands on a rocky peninsula, that joins Moidart by a narrow neck of sand. If this castle was repaired it might accommodate a party of 50 men, the repairs would cost at least 800 pounds; the walls of the building being quite insufficient, from the burning and tryings of the weather'.

DP094432 2011

Set on a coastal promontory to the south of Stonehaven, and bounded on all sides by sheer cliffs, Dunnottar Castle was known as one of the most secure and impregnable fortresses in Scotland. Perhaps because of this reputation, it regularly drew besieging armies to the head of the steep, narrow saddle that connects it to the mainland.

The Vikings sacked a Pictish stronghold built on this site in AD 890, and in 1296 William Wallace seized the castle from an English garrison. Three and a half centuries later, with Oliver Cromwell's armies on the march, the Scottish Crown Jewels were sent to Dunnottar for safety. The castle was soon under siege, and surrendered in 1652 – yet the English troops could find no trace of the crown, sceptre and sword of Scotland.

Instead the Jewels had been smuggled from the castle and buried beneath the pews of the nearby Kinneff church. According to one version of the story, they were lowered by rope from the cliffs to a girl collecting seaweed on the shore below, and then carried to the manse hidden in her creel.

ABOVE **DP114087** 2011

RIGHT **DP114084** 2011

Viewing the jagged, indented coastline of Scotland from above reveals an incredible variety of human intervention in the landscape – from ancient forts and farming settlements to the vast network of defensive installations created during the World Wars. At Whitberry Point, to the north-west of Dunbar, this bulb of land is known as 'St Baldred's Cradle'. Named after a sixth century Christian hermit, who lived in seclusion on a cell on the Bass Rock, the promontory has a raised mound of grass at its centre – buried underneath are the remains of an overgrown pillbox built during the second World War.

DP058320 2009

At Cape Wrath on the north-western tip of the Scottish mainland, the empty sands of Kearvaig Bay look out to the unbroken expanse of the north Atlantic. A solitary structure stands at the head of the bay amid cultivation remains and ruined walls. While much of this farmstead is thought to date back to the late eighteenth century, the building itself was constructed around 1877 as a shepherd's house for 'Balnakeil', an extensive sheep farm that ranged across the estates of the Duke of Sutherland. Today it has been renovated as a bothy and is used both by walkers and NATO soldiers conducting exercises on the Cape Wrath military training area.

SC961351 2004

Sometimes the remains of ancient coastal fortifications are so denuded as to become almost invisible. Here at the cliff-girt summit of the tiny islet of Eilean a' Ghaill in the Sound of Arisaig, the fragments of a wall and a stone-lined well are all that remain of a structure that would have commanded views over the sea to Rum, Eigg, Muck and the Ardnamurchan peninsula.

DP109049 2011

To the south of Machrihanish near the tip of the Mull of Kintyre, the steep-sided valley of Innean Glen descends to the sea. Stone-walled sheepfolds sit on hillside terraces, alongside the remains of what may once have been a farm building. Above the shoreline's rocky beach, a small cairn of stones and a simple wooden cross mark a 'sailor's grave'. In 1917, an unidentified body was washed ashore and buried by the local shepherd. The cross, which has been replaced several times over the years, bears the inscription 'God Knows'.

DP056842 2008

At the tip of the Ardnish peninsula, on a raised plateau overlooking Loch Ailort, are the remains of the deserted settlement of Peanmeanach. Roofless houses sit in a shallow crescent surrounded by the tracery of previous cultivation – evidence of a community that once tended cattle and sheep, and grew crops in the thin, acid soil of the coast.

Today one building remains in use, renovated in the 1970s as a bothy – a rest stop for walkers, who descend to the settlement by the 4 mile path that runs from the A830, passes Loch Doire a' Ghearrain, and follows an outlet stream to the shore.

LEFT **DP109057** 2011

ABOVE **DP109054** 2000

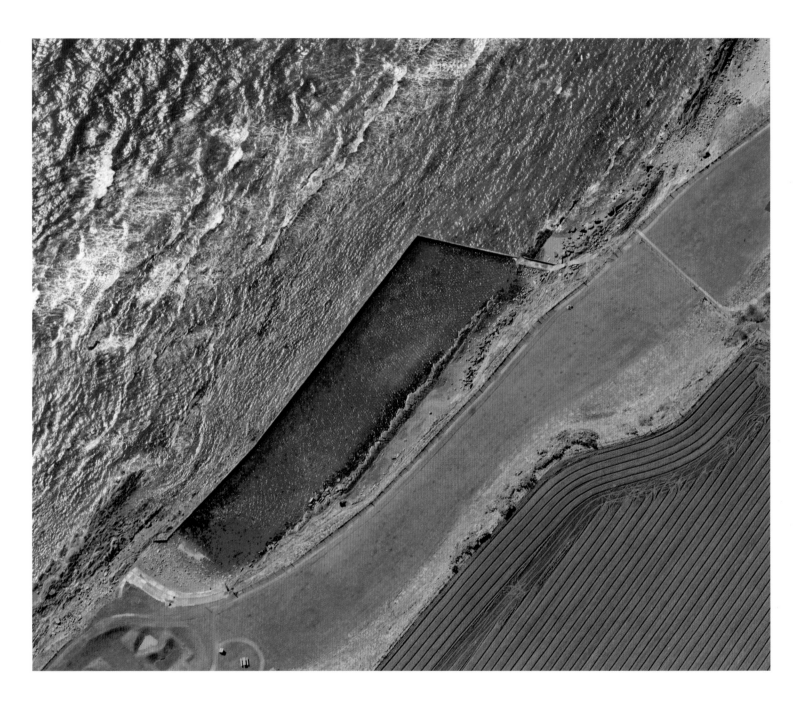

Some 100m long and 20m wide, the outdoor pool at St Monans in Fife is made out of one huge concrete basin, filled each day by tidal seawater. Now fallen into disuse, the pool was one of over 160 built at coastal resorts across Scotland in the 1930s. The popularity of outdoor pursuits and a belief in the medical benefits of bathing in salt water drove the trend for large-scale municipal constructions.

Yet, by the latter half of the twentieth century, the pools were already in decline. Today, many are unmaintained or demolished, architectural fragments of a very specific social fad, succumbing to erosion and ruin.

DP042587 2008

In a natural amphitheatre of steep-sided cliffs to the east of Macduff, the remains of the Tarlair Lido sit derelict and abandoned. This once spectacular Art Deco complex opened in the summer of 1931, and was made up of tidal swimming and boating pools surrounded by the sweeping terraces of curved, whitewash walkways.

Overlooking it all was an elegant, flat-roofed tea pavilion with changing rooms and kiosks. Although out of use since 1995, the pool complex was given category A-listing in 2007, and is now recognised as a structure of outstanding architectural and historic importance.

DP108838 2011

The twin routes of the road and railway 'to the Isles' run past the turquoise and gold estuary of the River Morar to sweep into the harbour of Mallaig. Just over a hundred years ago, this was a tiny settlement made up of a handful of thatched houses – most famous perhaps as a reputed landing point for Bonnie Prince Charlie when he escaped from Skye in July 1746, hidden beneath piles of plaid at the bottom of a boat. Although Lord Lovat oversaw the construction of a stone pier here in the mid nineteenth century – part of an 'improvement' scheme to develop the village as a fishing port – it was the arrival of the West Highland Railway in 1901 that truly transformed Mallaig. For a time a major industrial herring station and kippering centre, the harbour today is one of Scotland's most iconic transport hubs – a borderland between road, rail and ferry; a gateway to the Sound of Sleat, the Knoydart peninsula and the Isles.

LEFT **DP109027** 2011
RIGHT **DP109031** 2011

From the ivory sands of the Bay of Clachtoll, the B869 winds its way through the rocky Highland landscape of Assynt towards the major fishing port of Lochinver. Rising abruptly from the loch-strewn moorlands is the colossal cone of Suilven – a mountain made up of layers of Torridonian sandstone some 500 million years old.

This landscape has long been a place of pilgrimage for geologists – in 1912 luminaries from Norway, Switzerland, America and Russia stayed at the Inchnadamph Hotel on the banks of Loch Assynt, and heard pioneering new theories on mountain formation presented by British scientists Ben Peach and John Horne.
DP093071 2010

In the furthest reaches of the north-west Highlands, the ribbon of the A832 – pictured here passing the sands of Gruinard Bay – is built on top of one of the old 'Destitution Roads'. These routeways were constructed during a period of famine in the Highlands in the 1840s, providing employment for farmers in exchange for oatmeal rations. DP110036 2011

Beneath sheer cliffs on the western shore
of Loch Linnhe, the B8043 threads the
needle between rock and sea to reach
the tiny village of Kilmalieu. In the centre
of the left-hand image, a curved semi-circle
on the shoreline defines the remains of
a 'fish-trap'.

LEFT DP094394 2010
ABOVE DP094391 2010

Crossing the entrance to Loch Etive to the north east of Oban, Connel Bridge was constructed between 1898 and 1903 on the Ballachulish branch of the Caledonian Railway. For a time Connel was the second longest cantilever bridge in Europe – after the Forth Bridge – with its 500ft span avoiding the need to place any support piers in the strong currents of the tidal channel.

As early as 1914, it was modified to take both road and rail traffic. Yet just over 50 years later, the closure of the Ballachulish branch line saw the bridge adapted solely for cars.

DP070520 2009

The East Neuk of Fife's distinctive patchwork of farmlands and fishing villages stretches away into the distance. From a caravan park on the outskirts of St Monans, here the coastline runs through Pittenweem, Anstruther and Crail, before the 'Neuk' – or corner – turns westwards to St Andrews.

DP032884 2007

The cantilever shadow of the Forth Rail Bridge stretches out over the island of Inchgarvie. For centuries the nation's landscapes have presented unique challenges to engineers seeking to link communities through steep-sided Highland passes, or across lochs, rivers and inlets. Yet nothing had ever come close to the incredible scale and ambition of the Forth crossing. Built between 1883 and 1890, this 54,000 tonne, red steel behemoth, was held up as an icon of man's mastery of his environment.

As the bridge's designer Benjamin Baker wrote, 'The Engineers with their gigantic works sweep everything before them in this Victorian era.' Remarkably, had it not been for a dirty, debt-ridden war between two railway companies, the Forth Bridge might never have been built. The North British Railway bankrolled this huge undertaking to create an alternative east coast line to Aberdeen, breaking the Caledonian stranglehold over routes to northern Scotland. It was business and competition – not necessity – that created the world's largest railway bridge.

DP115240 2012

In August 1803, the poet Dorothy
Wordsworth wrote of her first sight of
the village of Inveraray on the shores
of Loch Fyne: 'We seemed now to be on
the edge of a very large, almost circular,
lake, the town of Inveraray before us, a line
of white buildings on a low promontory
right opposite and close to the water's edge;
the whole landscape a showy scene, and
bursting upon us at once ... It is so little
like an ordinary town, from the mixture
of regularity and irregularity in the
buildings ... A few steps more brought
us in view of the Castle a stately turreted
mansion, but with a modern air, standing
on a lawn, retired from the water, and
screened behind by woods covering the
sides of high hills to the top, and still
beyond, by bare mountains.' Inveraray was
'so little like an ordinary town' because
it was one of the earliest examples of a
planned town landscape, and had been
completely rebuilt some 60 years before
on the instructions of Archibald Campbell,
the third Duke of Argyll – a model
settlement to complement the Duke's new
model castle. Sir John Vanburgh, architect
of Blenheim Palace, is credited with
inspiring the initial design for Inveraray
Castle, but the Palladian-gothic pile that
eventually emerged in 1789 – after 43 years
of construction – was the product of a
number of architects, including Roger
Morris and William Adam, and Adam's
sons John and Robert.

LEFT DP099569 2011
TOP RIGHT DP105561 2011
BOTTOM RIGHT DP105552 2011

ABOVE

Nestled in a copse of trees, the white façade
of Kilmaronag House looks out over the
western end of Loch Etive towards Connel.
In the distance is Ben Cruachan – at 1,126m,
the highest peak in Argyll and Bute, and an
imposing gatekeeper to the western fringes
of the Grampian mountain range.
DP094713 2010

RIGHT

More of a palace than a country house,
Hopetoun sits in a 100 acre estate, 11 miles
to the east of Edinburgh. Standing on a
raised terrace, the house commands views
east along the Forth basin to the distant
peak of Ben Lomond, and west past the
twin spans of the road and rail bridges
to the widening Firth and the sea.
Originally designed by Sir William Bruce
at the very end of the seventeenth century,
the mansion was substantially remodelled
and enlarged by William Adam from 1721,
and completed in the year of his death in
1748. Adam's sons John and Robert also
had a hand in the reconstruction, and
with its extensive gardens and dramatic
frontage, it was not long before impressed
visitors were referring to Hopetoun as
the 'Scottish Versailles'. DP075459 2010

ABOVE

On a Moidart shoreline, looking out over the Sound of Arisaig to the Islands of Eigg and Rum, sits the estate of Roshven. In the mid nineteenth century, the dilapidated residence of the former laird was converted into a turreted, Scots Baronial towerhouse by the pre-eminent architect of the day, David Bryce. The new owners – Glasgow Professor of Mathematics Hugh Blackman and his artist wife Jemima – re-imagined the landscape as a romantic Highland getaway. The couple moved in prominent intellectual and artistic circles, and at Roshven they entertained some of the Victorian era's most celebrated figures, including John Ruskin, Anthony Trollope, Sir John Everett Millais, Benjamin Disraeli and Lord Kelvin.

DP109059 2011

RIGHT

Originally built by David Bryce in 1870 – and remodelled 24 years later by Sir Robert Lorimer after a fire – Ellary House looks out over a long, landscaped prospect to Loch Caolisport, the shores of Knapdale, and the distant Isle of Gigha.

DP108517 2011

On a peninsula jutting into the Moray Firth, Fort George is a striking tribute to the Jacobite Rebellion of 1745. Built in the aftermath of the uprising, it was a response to the fear that the Highlands could again muster its forces and march to war. After the old fort in Inverness was sacked before the Battle of Culloden, the new incarnation was designed to be impregnable – 40 acres in size, accommodation for 1,600 infantry, and enclosed by a mile of artillery fortifications. Completed in 1769, this was a monumental stamp of Hanoverian military authority in the landscape – yet it was never used for its intended purpose. Instead, it became a base to train young Highland recruits, before sending them across the world to fight for the Empire.

LEFT SC1019363 1999

ABOVE DP074869 2009

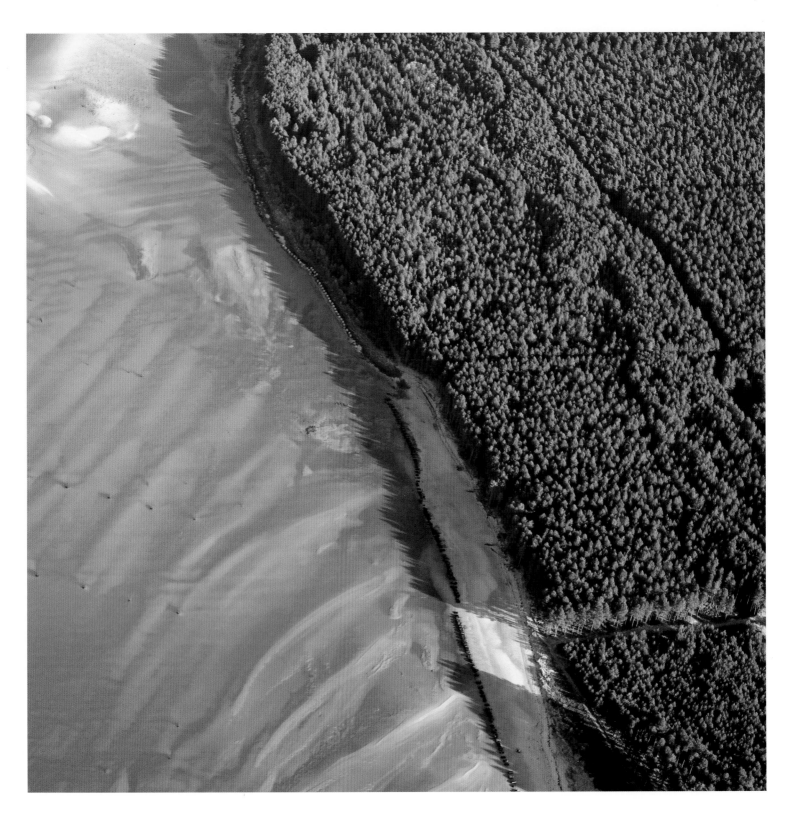

During the Second World War, the ever-present threat of sea-borne invasion saw the coastlines of Scotland transformed into the 'ramparts' of one massive island fortification. At Tentsmuir Forest on the southern banks of the Firth of Tay, the many fragments of these defences still remain embedded in the landscape.

The combination of deep water and a low, sandy coastline made this a prime position to attack, and saw a continuous stretch of anti-tank blocks – seen here following the tree-line – supported by observation posts and pillboxes.

Many of these were manned and constructed by Polish Units, who were based in an encampment set in the centre of the forest. A number of the blocks show the names of the soldiers who made them, their initials carved into the wet concrete.

DP036711 2007

Above a wide, sandy estuary at the mouth of the River Tyne to the west of Dunbar, a line of anti-tank blocks runs for nearly 2km through the Links Wood. Explosives were used to demolish many blocks after the war. However, the danger of concrete shrapnel embedding in trees has meant that many anti-tank defences in woodlands have remained untouched.

The series of paths – known as 'rides' – converging here on the wood's central clearing, are a landscape feature dating back to around 1700, when the sixth Earl of Haddington and his wife transformed their East Lothian estate of Tyninghame through extensive tree-planting.
DP058330 2009

At the beginning of the twentieth century, the British Admiralty identified the need for a major naval base on the east coast of Scotland. Using the natural, deep water basin at St Margaret's Hope on the Firth of Forth, Rosyth was developed both as a dockyard complex and as a 'garden city' to house workers involved in the building and maintenance of ships.

Construction began in 1909 – at peak involving over 6,000 men working round the clock – and by completion in 1917 the base covered an area of over 1,200 hectares. With the onset of the Cold War, Rosyth was developed as a refitting centre for Polaris nuclear submarines.

Although eventually closed as a naval base in 1996, the dockyard continues to operate today under commercial ownership.
DP051211 2008

A *Vanguard* class nuclear ballistic missile submarine with escort craft cruises through the Firth of Clyde near Dunoon. Since the 1960s, Britain's 'nuclear deterrent' submarine fleet has been based at the Faslane Naval Base, a vast military complex constructed above the deep waters of the Gare Loch.

DP062995 2009

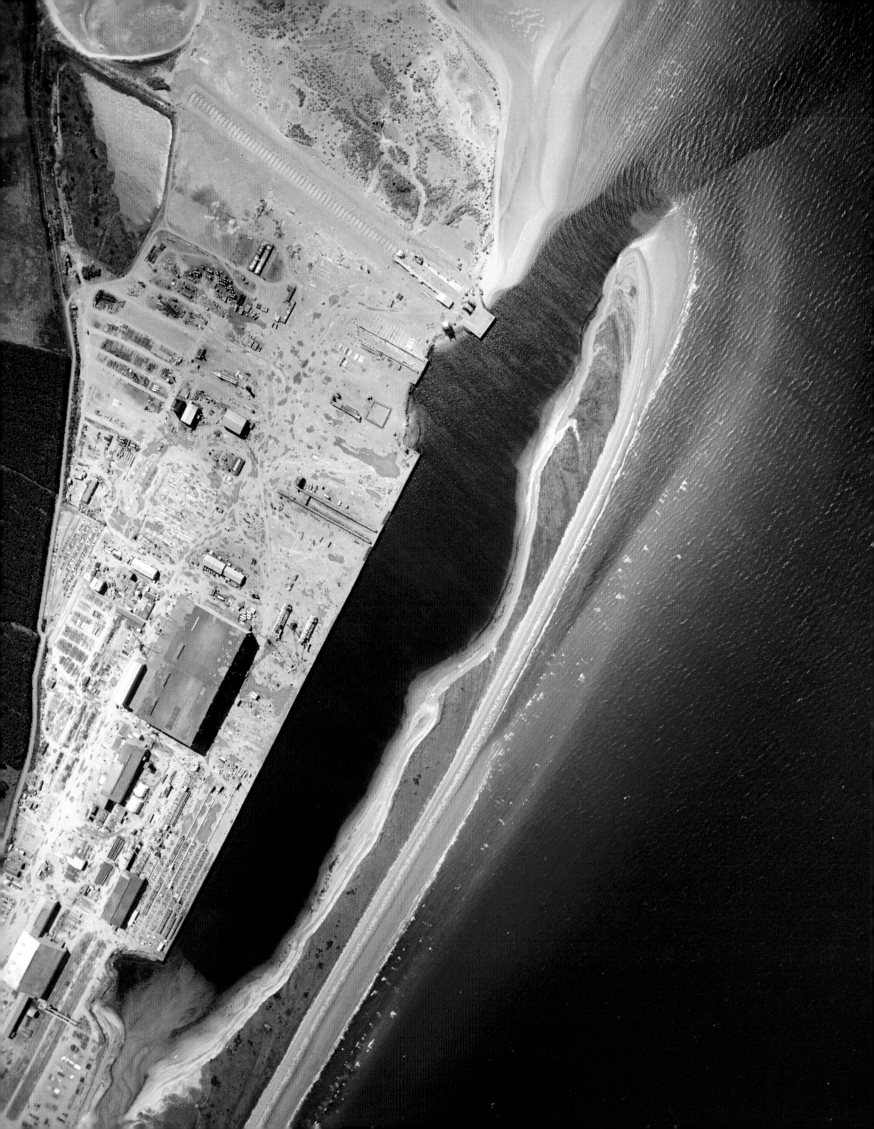

Situated on a sandy spit to the east of Nairn, the Ardersier Fabrication Yard was closed in 2002 after almost 30 years of activity. Over 3,000 people worked on the site, constructing offshore platforms for the oil industry.

The colossal fabrication building – seen here in the centre left – was over 100 feet high, covered 8 acres, and was, for a time, the largest structure of its kind in Europe.

SC1019347 1999

ABOVE

Surrounded by a patchwork farming landscape, the Nigg Fabrication Yard is built out onto a wedge of reclaimed land at the mouth of the Cromarty Firth. Today, rather than maintaining and repairing offshore oil platforms, the yard has been repurposed for the construction of wind turbines.

DP093512 2010

Above Loch Linnhe on the south coast of the Morvern peninsula, a vast chunk of the landscape has been removed. This is the work of the Glensanda superquarry, an industrial complex extracting Strontian granite from the mountain of Meall na h-Easaiche.

The 5 million tonnes of rock aggregate produced here each year are crushed in a vertical chute at the summit – known as a 'glory hole' – and then transferred by an underground conveyor belt running for 2km to a processing plant.

Loch Linnhe's deep coastal waters allow ocean-going container ships to berth alongside the huge mounds of stockpiled granite on the harbour side. Slowly but surely, an entire Scottish mountain is being quarried, crushed and exported around the world.

ABOVE DP111942 2011
RIGHT DP094385 2010

This links landscape, sweeping out into the North Sea from the town of St Andrews, is one of the places where golf is thought to have first been played. The origins of the sport date back to at least the fifteenth century, and it became so popular that it was banned in 1457 by an Act of Parliament passed by King James II – for fear it was distracting Scottish men from archery practice. In 1552, the local burgh granted Archbishop John Hamilton the right to establish a rabbit warren on the links, and at the same time enshrined the right of the townspeople to play golf among the grassland and dunes. Rabbit-farming and golf competed for the use of this land for centuries, until local landowner James Cheape of Strathtyrum purchased the wedge of coastline in 1821 and declared that he had 'saved the Links for golf'. Over 1,000 years ago, St Andrews was Scotland's religious epicentre: a burial ground for the relics of the nation's patron saint, and a site of pious pilgrimage. Today, this landscape is golf's 'holy place', a shrine to the game that attracts millions of enthusiasts from across the world.

DP100958 2011

The thin strip of the Balcombie Links golf course bends with the Fife coastline and stretches out to the very tip of the 'Neuk'. The course was designed by the legendary golfing figure 'Old' Tom Morris in 1895. Morris, the son of a St Andrews weaver, was the father of modern greenkeeping, a clubmaker, ballmaker and instructor, and enjoyed a career as one of the world's first golf professionals. He came second in the first ever Open Championship in 1860, and went on to win the title four times in subsequent years. Morris designed Balcombie for the Crail Golfing Society, the seventh oldest golf club in the world – established on 23 February 1786. There is evidence, however, that golf was played at Crail long before this first official meeting – records from the mid eighteenth century show that part of the nearby Sauchope farm was leased under the dual occupancy rights of 'grazing and golfing'.

DP100929 2011

Today, golf courses continue to be built throughout the landscapes of Scotland. Here at Menie Links – part of a long strip of beach that extends north-east along the coast from Aberdeen – a layout of tees, greens and fairways begins to emerge from the dunes.

DP114106 2011

As new technologies develop, the nature of
the coastal boundary is continually shifting.
Here, the wide expanse of the Solway Firth
becomes the site of a renewable energy
farm, with 60 giant turbines rising out
of the sea.
DP104653 2011

1
Sanna,
Ardnamurchan
Peninsula

2
Garmouth,
River Spey,
Moray Firth

3
Cove Harbour,
Berwickshire

4
St Abbs,
Berwickshire

5
Burghead,
Moray Firth

6
Eilean Loain,
Loch Sween

7
Tayvallich,
Loch a' Bhealich,
Loch Sween

8
Rhubodach,
Kyles of Bute

9
Inverie Bay,
Loch Nevis,
Knoydart

10
Kyle of Tongue,
Sutherland

11
Luce Bay,
Rhins of Galloway

12
Baldoon Sands,
Wigtown Bay

13
Dunskey Castle,
Rhins of Galloway

14
Greenan Castle,
South Ayrshire

15
Gylen Castle,
Kerrara,
Argyll

16
Castle Tioram,
Loch Moidart

17
Dunnottar Castle,
Aberdeenshire

17
Dunnottar Castle,
Aberdeenshire

18
St Baldred's
Cradle, Whitberry
Point, Dunbar

19
Kearvaig Bay,
Cape Wrath

20
Eilean a' Ghaill,
Sound of Arisaig

21
Innean Glen,
Mull of Kintyre

22
Peanmeanach,
Ardnish Peninsula,
Loch Ailort

22
Peanmeanach,
Ardnish Peninsula,
Loch Ailort

23
St Monans,
Fife

24
Tarlair Lido,
Macduff,
Aberdeenshire

25
Mallaig,
Lochaber

25
Mallaig,
Lochaber

26
Bay of Clachtoll,
Assynt

27
Gruinard Bay,
Wester Ross

28
Kilmalieu,
Loch Linnhe

28
Kilmalieu,
Loch Linnhe

29
Connel Bridge,
Loch Etive

30
The East Neuk,
Fife

31
The Forth Rail
Bridge,
Firth of Forth

32
Inveraray,
Loch Fyne

32
Inveraray,
Loch Fyne

32
Inveraray,
Loch Fyne

33
Kilmaronag
House,
Loch Etive

34
Hopetoun House,
Firth of Forth

35
Roshven House,
Moidart

36
Ellary House,
Loch Caolisport

37
Fort George,
Moray Firth

37
Fort George,
Moray Firth

38
Tentsmuir Forest,
Firth of Tay

39
Links Wood,
River Tyne,
Dunbar

40
Rosyth Dockyard,
Firth of Forth

41
Vanguard
submarine,
Firth of Clyde,
Dunoon

42
Ardersier
Fabrication Yard,
Nairn

43
Nigg
Fabrication Yard,
Cromarty Firth

44
Glensanda
Superquarry, Meall
na h-Easaiche,
Loch Linnhe

44
Glensanda
Superquarry, Meall
na h-Easaiche,
Loch Linnhe

45
St Andrews Links,
Fife

46
Balcombie Links,
Crail, Fife

47
Menie Links,
Aberdeenshire

48
Robin Rigg
Wind Farm,
Solway Firth

Coastlines Locations

A survey flight above Scotland's coast is a challenge for both the photographer and the pilot. There are 12,000km of torturously indented landscapes – always different depending on time and tide – to follow in the search for material remains. The long-forgotten rubble of tidal fish traps, broken down jetties and abandoned buildings are among the many fragments left by 10,000 years of human settlement.

Coastal erosion and rising sea levels mean that, with every passing year, we are in a race against time to record the evidence from our past before it is lost forever. But by tracing the course of this borderland from above, and by monitoring how it changes, we may also gather vital information to inform our future.

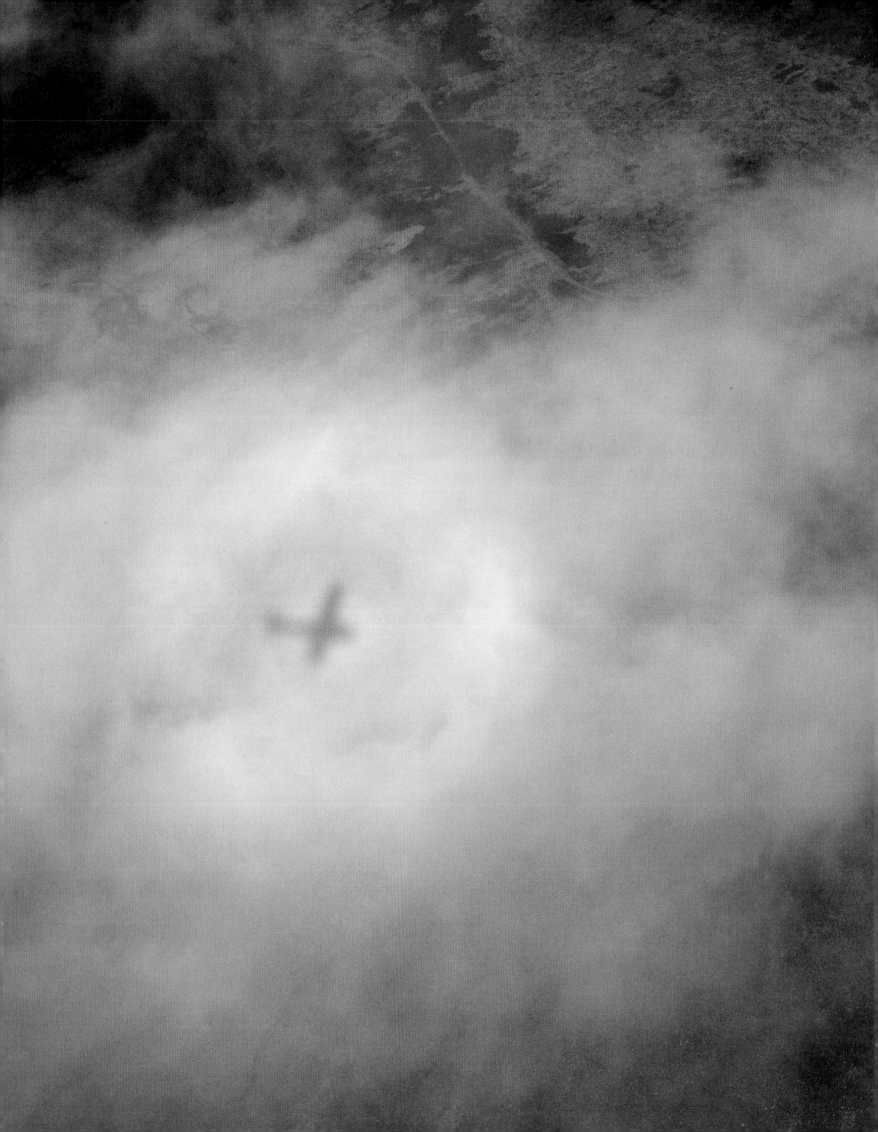

Scotland's National Collection of Aerial Photography

Held by the Royal Commission on the Ancient and Historical Monuments of Scotland (RCAHMS), the National Collection of Aerial Photography is one of the largest and most significant in the world. Often created for more immediate military or commercial purposes, these images have become an invaluable historical tool for everyone from archaeologists, geographers and conservationists to local and landscape historians. This unparalleled resource is made up of a number of distinct parts and is divided into two geographical areas – Scotland and worldwide.

IMAGERY OF SCOTLAND

We have has amassed 1.6 million images of Scotland from a number of different sources:

- Since 1976 RCAHMS has run an annual programme of aerial reconnaissance and photography to record the archaeology and buildings of Scotland, capturing changing urban and rural landscapes throughout the country, and leading to the discovery of thousands of new archaeological sites. Almost all of the imagery in this book comes from this collection – 150,000 images.
- The Aerofilms Collection contains some of the earliest aerial photographs ever taken of Scotland, and dates from 1919 up to the 1990s – 80,000 images
- The Royal Air Force Collection dates from the 1940s through to the 1990s, with more imagery continually added as it becomes declassified – 750,000 images.
- The Ordnance Survey Collection, produced to assist map-making, features imagery dating from 1955 through to 2001 – 500,000 images.
- The All Scotland Survey dates from 1987–9 and was commissioned by the then Scottish Office to assess land use – 17,000 images.

In addition to these, numerous smaller collections have also been added to the National Collection.

WORLDWIDE IMAGERY

In 2008, The Aerial Reconnaissance Archives (TARA) were entrusted to RCAHMS. Dating from 1938 onwards, these archives are made up of many millions of military intelligence photographs from around the world.

ACCESS

All images in this book, and a rapidly expanding selection of other photographs from the National Collection of Aerial Photography, are available to browse and buy online at rcahms.gov.uk and aerial.rcahms.gov.uk. Full access to the Collection is available in the RCAHMS public search room in Edinburgh.

On the way back to Kirkwall at the close of a day's flying, the aerial survey Cessna creates an optical illusion known as a 'Brocken spectre' – a magnified shadow in the mist, surrounded by a rainbow halo of diffracted light. Just a few hours in the skies can produce many weeks of work in the office, as new images have to be interpreted and catalogued, before being made accessible to the public through the RCAHMS online database. And in many ways, this is just the beginning. The National Collection of Aerial Photography is a vital, living record of our landscapes, and it can take each viewer on their own personal journeys of exploration. Fresh eyes provide new perceptions and perspectives – all of which have a role to play in informing our understanding of Scotland from above.

DP060193 2009

ACKNOWLEDGEMENTS

The preparation of this volume has benefited from
the input of many colleagues within RCAHMS.
These include Robert Adam, Rebecca Bailey, Steve Boyle,
Oliver Brookes, Alasdair Burns, Tania Dron, Dave Cowley,
Angela Gannon, George Geddes, Simon Green, Alex Hale,
Elaine Johnston, Bryony Jackson, Kevin Macleod,
Anne Martin, Alan Potts and Derek Smart.
Thanks are also due to Ronnie Cowan, Pam Scholefield,
Jack Stevenson, Mairi Sutherland, Martin Tilley, and
Agnieska Urbanska.

Index